FROM ABRAHAM TO ARMAGEDDON

The Convergence of Current Events, Bible Prophecy and Islam

FROM ABRAHAM TO ARMAGEDDON

The Convergence of Current Events, Bible Prophecy and Islam

T.W. TRAMM

TW
PRESS

For Mom

Acknowledgements

I would like to acknowledge the authors whose works served as my primary resource with respect to the role that Islam clearly plays in the fulfillment of Bible prophecy: Joel Richardson and Walid Shoebat. Several chapters of this book draw heavily upon their extensive knowledge in the fields of both Islamic and biblical eschatology. Any one of their books, which are listed in the bibliography, come highly recommended for those wishing to do further reading on the topic.

Also, special thanks to Nadia, and to my entire family, for all of the help and encouragement along the way.

Most of all, I would like to thank God—for many things, of course, but here, particularly, for opening my eyes to the incredible things that are happening in our time.

A Word About Muslims

This book will focus on aspects of Islam that may cast Muslims in an unflattering light. However, it is not my intention to incite hatred or disrespect toward Muslims. For this reason, I would like to take a moment to draw a distinction between the *ideology* that is Islam and the *individual* who calls himself "Muslim."

As with any religion, there are varying degrees of commitment among those of the Islamic faith. Obviously, not all Muslims are terrorists, and many wish to have no part in the "holy war" that is currently being waged in the name of Islam. The truth is that most Muslims we encounter likely share interests and ambitions in life that are similar to our own.

Additionally, like those of us who practice other faiths, the majority of Muslims were born into their religion, and in closed Islamic societies many have never had the opportunity to study anything other than the Koran. For the Muslims who do sense the shortcomings of Islam and begin to question their religion, there are few options—as those found guilty of apostasy in Islamic countries are frequently thrown into prison, or executed.

Having clarified that the intent of this book is not to demonize Muslims as individuals, it should be noted that no attempt will be made at political correctness with respect to the *religion* of Islam.

The reality today is that the mainstream media has largely sidestepped the truth in their underreporting of Islam's true ideologies. This failure to expose the underlying motives and objectives of Islam has only enabled its more radical adherents to promulgate evil and bloodshed under the guise of "a religion of peace."

In the years since 9/11, more and more westerners have begun to peel back the veneer that conceals the true face of Islam; what is revealed is a dark and oppressive belief system that entertains aspirations of world domination.

Islam has a long and well-documented history of violence and cruelty—most of it carried out in observance of the Koran—as well as the other teachings of its founder, Muhammed. Yet, there is much more to this story, as you will see.

Preface

I t is my hope that this will not be taken as a hysterical shout from the rooftops that "the world is coming to an end!" I am not suggesting that anyone sell all that they own, or start hoarding food and move to a cave in the hills. To be frank, this book was written with full awareness that most people regard the topic of the *end times*—as well as those who profess interest—with a sense of wariness often reserved for the odd individual who is talking to himself on the street corner or, perhaps, the stray dog that appears to be foaming at the mouth.

Nonetheless, the implications of the realities addressed here are of such magnitude that I could not sleep soundly without having made an attempt to share them with those who would not normally delve into such topics.

In the following pages, some assertions will be made—namely that we are living in the days referred to by students of prophecy as the "end times." Indeed, the very premise of this book is based on the notion. Still, no attempt is made to forecast a date for the Second Coming of Christ. My intention is simply to point the way toward some signs and raise some questions for the reader to consider.

Thus, what follows is essentially a crash course in Islamic history, Bible prophecy, and current events, as they relate to eschatology, or the "study of the end times." It is a distillation of facts and data gleaned from the Bible, as well as dozens of current books and articles that explore the topics of end-times prophecy and the religion of Islam.

This book was written for the "non-Bible scholar" who desires to know the truth concerning the end times but who has been discouraged by the host of contradictory teachings that flood the book-shelves and airwaves today.

The observations made herein are based on sound, verifiable data. Where Scripture is referenced, it is done so with respect to its proper context within the Bible. Moreover, there has been no attempt to twist or distort the meaning of any passage in order to force conformity to the ideas presented.

Even so, I ask that the reader not take anything suggested here for granted but to test everything for themselves by reading the referenced verses within the full framework of the Bible and also by verifying the historical data that is cited.

The Islamic role in the end times is a broad topic; therefore, we will approach it much like one might undertake the assembly of a large puzzle: methodically laying out the individual pieces and then proceeding to fit them together, until an overall picture begins to emerge. It is in many ways a startling picture, but it is also one which reminds us that God is in control, as the ancient Bible prophecies begin to unfold before our eyes.

Contents

Part V: The Current State of Affairs

Introduction

It has been said that *"For those who want to believe, no facts are necessary, but for those who do not, no amount of evidence will ever be enough."* This statement highlights what is, perhaps, one of life's most simple truths: There are some who require little or no proof in order to accept something as fact, while others cannot see beyond their own preconceived notions and are consequently *blinded* by what they already *know* to be the true.

Fortunately, many of us fall somewhere in-between these two extremes, relying on good old-fashioned common sense, as well as a reasonable amount of data from which to draw upon, as we solve life's puzzles.

Our legal system is, of course, grounded in this same reasoning. For instance, in a civil case, a "preponderance of evidence" is considered sufficient to enable the rendering of a sound judgment on any given matter.

It is with this in mind that I invite the reader to consider some very compelling evidence: It involves a phenomenon that many students of the Bible have only begun to awaken to and is radically changing the way in which many view the religion of Islam.

As recently as a century ago, the region that we generally refer to as the "Middle East" was dominated by an Islamic Empire, which, at the time, was united under a series of monocratic leaders known as "Caliphs." Spanning much of Southeastern Europe, the Middle East, and North Africa, this empire was extraordinarily immense and, many would add, equally as oppressive.

At the end of World War One, after more than six centuries of conquest, the Ottoman Empire collapsed, reducing this once great kingdom to a scattering of feuding Muslim states. The Islamic world has since been one without unity, as well as the authority and prestige that accompany it. However, in light of what the Bible forecasts, it appears that this may not be the case forever.

Many, today, would be surprised to learn that the demise of the Islamic Empire, as well as its ultimate regeneration into a malevolent superpower, is chronicled in the pages of the Bible. In fact, Islam itself is referenced throughout the Scriptures; though not mentioned by name, the parallels are indisputable. The Bible characterizes a worldwide *"worship"* movement that attempts to impose its rule, its laws, and its god, onto the inhabitants of the earth. According to the Scriptures, this satanically inspired governing system will persecute Christians and Jews—forcing all to submit to *"the beast,"* while eliminating those who will not.

Most people do not realize that we are currently witnessing a phenomenon that is unparalleled throughout all of history. Due, in large part, to the vast sums of oil money that have been coursing into the Middle East for decades—as well as a religion that requires its adherents to dominate the world for Allah—the once apparently lifeless Islamic Empire is slowly being brought back from the brink of extinction and is preparing to be reborn.

The world will one day marvel, as a coalition of Islamic nations takes shape, reuniting the Muslim world and giving rise to a *new* Islamic Empire. Shortly after the emergence of this new kingdom, it will fall under the rule of a highly venerated Muslim leader; though, most in those days will not grasp the significance of this.

Today, many Muslims are convinced that Islam's destiny of world domination is drawing ever closer, and they are correct. Islam is certain to become a predominating force in the years ahead, and will bring about a time of chaos and destruction the likes of which mankind has yet to see.

The horrific events of those days will be recognized by many Christians as the "great tribulation." The Bible tells us that these things must take place in the years immediately preceding the glorious return of Jesus Christ and the end of history as we know it.

PART I

Laying the Groundwork

In order to understand the present or, for that matter, the future, with respect to Bible Prophecy, one must know a little about the past; the past meaning not fifty or sixty years ago but millennia ago. This is how far back in history one must travel in order to pinpoint the genesis of what is currently taking shape in the Middle East and, in fact, the world today. Yet, it is a journey well worthwhile, as a basic understanding of the beginnings will greatly enhance our appreciation of how this remarkable sequence of events is going to culminate.

With this in mind, the first of the two brief chapters that make up part one of this book will be dedicated to tracing the origins of the Jewish and Arabic peoples—ultimately revealing the very starting point of the hostility toward Israel and, indeed, the true underpinnings of today's conflict. We will then fast forward 2,600 years to the life of Muhammed and the dark revelations that led to the birth of a new religion, Islam. It is here that we learn how relations in the Middle East went from sometimes *problematic*, to downright *ugly*.

Having mapped out the first part of our course, let us begin to lay the all-important groundwork for this most incredible story.

ONE

And Esau hated Jacob because of the blessing wherewith his father blessed him: and Esau said in his heart, The days of mourning for my father are at hand; then will I slay my brother Jacob.

—Genesis 27:14

Origins

I t would be nearly impossible to read a newspaper or watch the news today without stumbling upon at least a handful of stories that involve the Middle East, Israel, or the surrounding turmoil. Despite involving a relatively small land area and number of casualties, the ongoing unrest in the region has been the focus of worldwide media and diplomatic attention for decades.

This is due, in part, to the fact that many elsewhere in the world feel drawn into this conflict for various reasons. These may range from the purely ideological—such as cultural and religious ties with Islam, Christianity, or Judaism—to the strictly financial or politically motivated interests of certain parties or nations.[1]

Some have even suggested that it is the constant exposure to the coverage put forth by the Western media and the Arab press that fuels the seemingly global interest in the Middle East. Unfortunately, much of this coverage imparts a biased, politicized view of what the mainstream believes is driving the Islamic hatred of the Jews, and also the West.

Why All of the Fighting?

Perhaps hundreds, if not thousands, of books have been written on the subject of the Arab-Israeli conflict—each offering an assorted and complex array of explanations for its prolonged existence. For our purposes, however, rather than attempting to delve into the subtle nuances of each supposed cause, we are simply going to touch on today's generally accepted points of contention before going straight to the heart of what underlies them all.

Let us get started, then, with some basics:

The first Arab-Israeli war began on May 15, 1948. A mere twenty four hours had passed since Israel's declaration of statehood, when five Arab nations invaded, publicly declaring their intention to slaughter all of the Jews and "drive them into the sea." This war, of course, resulted in a victory for Israel and the displacement of thousands of Arab Palestinians who had been living within its borders. Thus was born the infamous "Palestinian Issue."

Sadly, if the Arab leaders had not flatly rejected an earlier UN resolution, which called for the establishment of two states in Palestine (one Arab and one Jewish), there would have been no dislocation in the first place; but rather than compromise, they chose to attack—with the objective of strangling Israel at birth. For the Arabs, the existence of a Jewish state in their midst was simply unacceptable.

Aside from the still ongoing "displaced Palestinian Issue," the current areas of dispute are actually lands that Israel captured from Egypt, Jordan, and Syria during the 1967 Six-Day War; they include the West Bank, the Golan Heights, East Jerusalem, and specifically the area known as the "Temple Mount."

Both Muslims and Jews claim sovereignty over the site of the Temple Mount. The Jews contend ownership as it was the site of the Jewish Temple, which was the very center of ancient Jewish worship. It housed the "Holy of Holies," which contained the Ark of the Covenant, and was said to be the area upon which God's "presence" dwelt.

Originally built in 967 B.C., the Temple was destroyed nearly four centuries later by the Babylonians. A second temple, rebuilt in 516 B.C., was subsequently demolished in the siege of Jerusalem by the Romans in 70 A.D., leaving only the bare "mount" standing.

This same area also holds great significance to Muslims. Referred to as the "Noble sanctuary," it is considered to be the "third holiest" site in all of Islam. It is the location of two major Muslim religious shrines: the Dome of the Rock, built circa 690 A.D., and the Al-Aqsa Mosque, built around 710 A.D.

The Al-Aqsa Mosque was purportedly built as a marker to the

location that Muslims believe Muhammad, the founder of Islam, ascended to heaven.

Incidentally, most Palestinian leaders routinely deny the well-documented Jewish ties to the Temple Mount. In fact, in spite of overwhelming archaeological evidence, many claim that the temples never existed.[2]

Nonetheless, while tensions have undoubtedly escalated since the Jewish recapturing of Jerusalem in 1967, the contested ownership of these holy sites, or even the current Iraq War, cannot be faulted as the only sources of discord in the region.

"Behold, I will make Jerusalem a cup of trembling unto all the people round about…"

Many of us who watch the Middle East wonder why the ongoing disputes never seem to reach any kind of resolution. Despite peace talks, compromises on the part of the Israelis, and the best attempts at mediation by other nations, the hostility continues. To be sure, never has such a small piece of land aroused such indignation on the part of so many, or been so globally divisive, as Israel.

Considering this, it seems that aside from the disputed areas of land, there must be something else fueling all of the animosity that is directed toward this tiny nation. Could it be that the true source of hostility actually stems from something more deeply rooted?

A Distinguished Family Tree

It is impossible to understand the present-day Middle East without knowledge of Abraham and his descendants. The three principal religions that emanate from the area: Judaism, Christianity and Islam, all trace their spiritual roots back to him. The chief historical figures behind these religions: Moses, Jesus Christ, and Muhammad, were all direct descendants of Abraham.

In this chapter, we are going to take a very brief look at the descendants of Abraham—this, in order to gain a sense of what has transpired throughout history to place them at center stage in an area of the world that seems to be in eternal turmoil.

Before we begin, however, for those who are already getting an uneasy feeling that what follows is an in-depth study of Bible genealogy, rest assured; we will not be plodding through a lengthy list of Bible patriarchs, or studying the intricacies of "who begat whom," but will simply be taking note of two key events involving Abraham's sons and grandsons: the birth of a younger brother and the turning over of a birth rite. Knowledge of these seemingly ordinary family happenings will serve to shed some much-needed light on the Arab-Israeli conflict, as well as provide an eye-opening perspective with regard to what we see playing out in the Middle East today.

The Patriarch

Abraham was born in the Tigris-Euphrates Valley region, in the area we know as Iraq, almost four thousand years ago. He was already advanced in age (ninety-nine years old) at the time God chose to enter into an everlasting covenant with him, promising to bring forth a *multitude of nations* from his seed.

It was through Abraham and the descendants of his son, Isaac (the Jews), that God would set up His model to the rest of the world. We see this model exhibited throughout the Bible, as the Scriptures reveal how God has chosen to deal with Abraham's descendants—both in how He has rewarded them and, also, judged them, according to their obedience to His Word. This has served as the ultimate lesson from which man is to gain understanding of how God operates and how He has approached his dealings with humankind throughout history.

"...And in your seed all the nations of the earth shall be blessed;"

Even more than a mere *example* to the world, God would use Abraham's descendants as the very *vehicle* of salvation for the rest

8

of mankind. God's Word (the Bible) would be given to, and recorded by, the Hebrew Prophets, for the benefit of all humanity.

Further still, it was, of course, the Jewish blood line through which Jesus Christ, God's ultimate salvation for man, would be born.

Clearly, the importance of God choosing Abraham to be the very point of origin for so many world-changing events—both historical and those yet to come—cannot be overstated.

With these things in mind, let us now take a look at how Abraham and his sons affected the course of history and, ultimately, the destiny of mankind, forever.

First Contact

Our story begins with God speaking to Abram: "…*Get out of your country, from your family and from your father's house, to a land that I will show you. I will make you a great nation; I will bless you and make your name great; and you shall be a blessing*" (*Genesis 12:1, 2*).

In Genesis 12:4 we find that Abram obeys what God has told him: "*So Abram departed as the LORD had spoken to him…*" Hebrews 11:8 adds: "*And he went out, not knowing where he was going.*"

On arriving in the new land, God promised Abram that He would give the land to his descendants: "*And the LORD said to Abram,…"Lift your eyes now and look from the place where you are—northward, southward, eastward, and westward; for all the land which you see I give to you and your descendants forever*" (*Genesis 13:14, 15*). In verse 16, God adds: "*And I will make your descendants as the dust of the earth; so that if a man could number the dust of the earth, then your descendants also could be numbered.*"

Significantly, God later changed Abram's name to *Abraham*. His earlier name meant "high (exalted) father." God renamed him "father of a multitude," saying, "*I will make you exceedingly fruit-*

ful; and I will make nations of you, and kings shall come from you" *(Genesis 17:6).*

In addition, God promised Abraham that he would have an heir: *"one who will come from your own body"* *(Genesis 15:4).*

After ten years had passed and no child had been born, Abraham's wife, Sarah, became impatient. Because of her impatience, and perhaps a lack of faith in God's promise, she bid Abraham to take the Egyptian handmaid, Hagar, and produce a child by her.

Abraham's First Son: Ishmael

"So he went in to Hagar, and she conceived. And when she saw that she had conceived, her mistress became despised in her eyes" *(Genesis 16:4).*

Hagar's pregnancy gave rise to strong feelings of superiority toward Abraham's wife, Sarah. The relationship between Sarah and Hagar quickly deteriorated, and when Hagar could no longer endure it, she fled into the desert.

The Bible tells us that the *"angel of the LORD"* found Hagar in the wilderness and instructed her to return home. At the same time, He reassured her that her son would *also* have many descendants— but descendants with traits that would be evident throughout their history: *"I will so increase your descendants that they will be too numerous to count…You are now with child and you will have a son. You shall name him Ishmael (God hears) for the LORD has heard of your misery. He will be a wild donkey of a man; his hand will be against everyone and everyone's hand against him, and he will live in hostility toward all his brothers"* *(Genesis 16:10-12).*

This description of Hagar's descendants is significant, as many of today's Arabs are *Ishmaelites*—descendants of this same Ishmael. In fact, Muhammad, the founder of Islam, was descended from one of the twelve sons of Ishmael.

Today, twenty-two nations in the Middle East and North Africa are Arabic, many of whom are descendants of Ishmael's, and who are also adherents to Muhammed's religion, Islam.[3]

Abraham's Second Son: Isaac

Fourteen years after the birth of Ishmael, God blessed Abraham with another son—this time by his *wife*, Sarah. God told them to name their son "Isaac," meaning *laughter*, for the incredulous reaction that they had when told they would have a son at their advanced age, as well as the joy that he would later bring to his parents.

It is Isaac, Abraham's second son, who would eventually father Jacob, also named *Israel* (the father of the Israelites). Thus, we see that Ishmael's and Isaac's descendants (the Arabs and the Jews) are, in fact, cousins.[4]

The Roots of an Ancient Rivalry Are Formed

Significantly, the birth of Isaac would prove to be a source of friction within Abraham's family. It cannot be said that Ishmael hated his new brother Isaac, but after fourteen years as an only child, Isaac's arrival fundamentally changed Ishmael's relationship with his father, Abraham. As a result, Ishmael began to harbor feelings of envy and rivalry toward his half-brother.[5]

Notably, these negative feelings did not die out with Ishmael, or his immediate offspring, but would survive to be passed down through the centuries, becoming deeply ingrained into the consciousness of his descendants.

Sarah Rejects Ishmael

As Isaac matures, the plot thickens: "*So the child (Isaac) grew and was weaned. And Abraham made a great feast on the same day that Isaac was weaned. And Sarah saw the son of Hagar (Ishmael) whom she had borne to Abraham, scoffing. Therefore she said to Abraham; 'Cast out this bondwoman and her son; for the son of this bondwoman shall not be heir with my son, namely with Isaac' (Genesis 21:8-10).*

Sarah's rejection of Ishmael greatly displeased Abraham, who had grown to love him. Nevertheless, God instructs Abraham to do as Sarah had asked: "...*Whatever Sarah has said to you, listen to her voice; for in Isaac your seed shall be called*" (Genesis 21:12).

God made it clear that *Isaac* was the son through whom He would fulfill his covenant with Abraham. However, knowing that Abraham loved both of his sons, God reassures him with regard to Ishmael's future: "*Yet I will also make a nation of the son of the bondwoman, because he is your seed*" (Genesis 21:13).

Later, we learn that Ishmael goes on to thrive in the desert and, in due course, takes an Egyptian woman to be his wife: "*And God was with the lad; and he grew, and dwelt in the wilderness, and became an archer. And he dwelt in the wilderness of Paran: and his mother took him a wife out of the land of Egypt*" (Genesis 21:20, 21).

Isaac's Two Sons—and the Loss of a Birth Rite

Isaac also eventually grew to take a wife (Rebekah), and she bore him twins: two sons that would be named Jacob and Esau. Even before they were born, "*the children struggled together within her*" (Genesis 25:22).

God explained to Rebekah: "*...two nations are in thy womb, and two manner of people shall be separated from thy bowels; and the one people shall be stronger than the other people; and the elder shall serve the younger*" (Genesis 25:23).

Each of these twins was to father a great nation: a blessing from God to Abraham's grandsons.

Yet, out of this good fortune, additional family complications would arise: Normally, the *first-born* would receive the birthright, but in this case, it was to be different. The Bible records that Esau, who was technically the first-born of the twins, sold his birthright to Jacob (Israel) for a bowl of lentil stew—demonstrating how little it meant to him.

Sometime later, Jacob received the birthright blessing that Esau had given up. For this, Esau "*hated*" Jacob.

Once more, the consequences of this apparently pivotal event are with us to this day. The descendants of Esau eventually intermarried with Ishmael's offspring—their combined bitterness and resentment toward Jacob's (Israel's) descendants further intensifying down through the generations.[6]

The rift that formed between these two brothers is actually referred to by some scholars as a defining moment in the history of the Middle East, as the notion that Esau was "cheated" out of his birth rite remains as a primary source of bitterness among the Arabic people.

In light of this, we see that while the hostility and conflict between the Jews and Arabs is often framed as being very complex in nature, it can also be boiled down to terms that any family, who has experienced the woes of sibling rivalry, might readily relate to.

The Eternal Family Feud

As we wrap up our brief study of Abraham's descendants, we come away with an invaluable insight into what is often overlooked by the mainstream today. Clearly, this ongoing conflict is the result of much more than some disputed areas of land or contested holy sites. It is rooted in the very origins of the Arab & Jewish peoples, going back nearly four thousand years. Indeed, the two branches of Abraham's offspring—the descendants born of his wife, Sarah (the Jews), and those born of the Egyptian maid, Hagar (the Ishmaelites)—are, to this day, engaged in a *"struggle"* with one another.

For those living in Westernized cultures, it may be difficult to imagine how a people could cling to these ancient feelings of animosity for centuries—let alone thousands of years—but this is, in fact, the reality for the Arab people. The bitterness toward the Jews has been deeply engrained as part of the Arabic culture and heritage and is ultimately at the root of what we see playing out in the Middle East today.

Still, there is more to the story of ongoing Arab-Israeli conflict than just this ancient feud. Beginning in the seventh century A.D., the advent of a new religion would do much to fan the flames of hatred. This religion, Islam, will be the focus of our next chapter.

Conclusion

Here, we have only begun to scratch the surface of the long and complex history of the Arabic and Jewish peoples, yet we are more informed than most as to the basic underpinnings of the Arab hostility toward Israel.

Today, in spite of the ripple effects that these ancient and current conflicts are having on the world, some may still question why one should be concerned with the past—let alone the future—of the Arabs and the Jews.

While the rationale will become evident as we progress, it can, for now, be summed up as follows: God is using both of these nations to carry out His plans for the closing of this age and the ushering in of a new one, as each of them are destined to play a pivotal role in the events leading up to the return of Christ. We can therefore be certain that the descendants of Abraham will remain at center stage until the curtain goes up on the final act of history.

TWO

"When the Prophet returned from the Trench, laid down his arms and took a bath, Gabriel came to him covered in dust. "Why have you laid down your sword? We angels have not set them down yet. It's time to go out against them.' The Prophet said, 'Where to go?' Gabriel said, 'This way,' pointing towards the Qurayza. So the Prophet went out to besiege them."

—Bukhari: V5B59N443-8

Islam: A Brief History

The story of Islam begins at the dawn of the seventh century A.D. in the Arabian Desert: a harsh and unforgiving wasteland, which, at the time, was sparsely dotted with cities and towns.

The ancient city of Mecca was emerging as an important commercial and religious center. Situated at the southwestern coast of the Red Sea, it was at the cross roads of a major trading route where goods destined for what is now Syria and Iraq would be loaded onto caravans.[1]

Following some extended periods of seclusion and meditation in the mountains surrounding Mecca, a young Arab travel merchant named Muhammed would claim to have been visited by an angel in an isolated cave at mount Hira. It was from this singular event that a new and world-changing religion would spring forth.

The Father of Islam

Born in Mecca in the year 570 A.D., Muhammed grew up poor and orphaned on the margins of society. He lived in a barren and desolate region, which was primarily controlled by tribal chiefs and trading merchants.

Muhammed did not experience much in the way of stability in his younger years. He never knew his father, and was a mere six years old at the time that his mother passed away. Muhammed's grandfather temporarily took charge of raising him, but he too, died soon thereafter. Subsequently, an uncle named Abu Talib adopted young Muhammed and raised him as his own son until he reached maturity.[2]

It is widely believed by Muslim scholars that Muhammad did not receive any formal education and thus began working with the caravans at a young age. It was while working as a trader that Muhammad came to know the widow Khadija, who was the owner of the caravan company for which he worked.

At the age of twenty-five, Muhammad married Khadija, who, at the time, was fifteen years his senior. Khadija bore Muhammed six children, and it is said that they had a strong marriage, up until the time of her death in 619 A.D.

Soon after Khadija's death Muhammad remarried. However, unlike his former marriage, he chose to take multiple wives—some reports say as many as nine.[3]

Muhammed's First Revelation

The lifestyle afforded by his wife Khadija's wealth allowed Muhammed the opportunity to wander off occasionally for periods of "meditation and contemplation." At some point, he began retreating to a cave in the surrounding mountains near Mecca.[4]

According to the Islamic traditions, it was here, at age forty, in the month of Ramadan, that Muhammed received his first "revelation." The following is a popular version of this encounter, in which the angel Gabriel is said to have brought him the command of god:

"The commencement of divine inspiration to Allah's Messenger was in the form of dreams that came true like a bright light. The Prophet loved the seclusion of a cave in Hira. The angel came to him and asked him to read. The Prophet replied, 'I do not know how to read.' The Prophet added, 'Then the angel caught me forcefully and pressed me so hard that I could not bear it any more. He released me and asked me to read. I replied, "I do not know how to read." Thereupon he caught me again and pressed me till I could not bear it any more. He asked me to read but I replied, "I do not know how to read or what shall I read?" Thereupon he caught me for the third time and pressed me, "Read in the name of your Lord who has created man from a clot. Read! Your Lord is the most generous." Then the Apostle returned from that experience; the muscles between his neck and shoulders were trembling, and his heart beating severely. He went to Khadija and cried, 'Cover me! Cover me.' She did until his fear subsided. He said, 'What's wrong with me? I am afraid that something bad has happened to me...'"[5]

Plagued by Uncertainty

Needless to say, Muhammed's first encounter with this angelic being was a profoundly disturbing experience. In fact, he was actually afraid that he had been possessed by a demon; though his wife, Khadija, assured him that it was not so.[6]

In spite of this reassurance, Muhammed continued to be plagued by doubts and fear. The Islamic traditions state that he would go for three years without further revelation from the angel—all the while battling a nagging depression.[7]

Finally, Muhammed became suicidal and was on his way to throw himself from a cliff to escape his despair, when the angel Gabriel suddenly appeared on the horizon and assured him that he was, indeed, the "prophet of Allah."[8]

Although Muhammed's spirits were greatly lifted by this latest revelation, it is noted in some accounts that he was deathly afraid at the angel's appearance. Muhammed succinctly describes one such encounter: "*I was walking one day when I saw the angel who used to come to me at Hira. I was terror stricken by him*" (Tabari VI:76).

Nonetheless, from this point forward the revelations began to come to Muhammed on an ever more frequent basis—continuing up until the time of his death, twenty-three years later.[9]

The First Convert

During the first few years of revelation, Muhammed would convey the "words of Allah" exclusively to his family and friends. It is perhaps not surprising, then, that according to many scholars, the first person to convert to Islam was Muhammed's wife, Khadija. To be sure, Khadija is believed to have been an important source of influence and support for Muhammed. The traditions seem to reinforce this notion, relating that *"All her wealth was spent in the way of Allah, helping to spread the message of her husband..."*[10]

As for Muhammed's later wives, they also believed him to be a prophet of Allah—in part, because he would sometimes appear to enter epileptic frenzies while receiving revelation.

Yet, in spite of his wives' confidence in the matter, Muhammed still entertained feelings of self doubt—going through prolonged periods in which he thought that he might be mad, or possessed by a demon.

The Precarious Prophet

As Muhammed grew more confident in his message, he began to denounce the polytheism (multiple idol worship) of his forefathers and fellow Arabs—openly preaching his new doctrine of a *singular* god in his hometown of Mecca. As a consequence of this new teaching, Muhammed was ridiculed and labeled a "madman" by some.[11]

Under threats of death, he moved to Medina with a small band of followers, where he found a large group of Jews who also believed in "one God." His following increased, but when the Jews noticed all of the contradictions between Muhammed's teachings and their Torah, he was quickly rejected as a prophet. This greatly offended Muhammed.[12]

Economically uprooted, and with no available profession beside that of arms, the Muslim migrants turned to raiding Meccan caravans for their livelihood, in this manner initiating armed conflict between the Muslims and Mecca.[13]

Still stinging from the rejection of his own hometown and tribe, it was at Medina that Muhammad's message became more intolerant and ruthless—particularly as he gained power.[14]

Muhammed Re-claims Mecca as His Own

The tide would soon turn in Muhammed's favor, as he began experiencing success with uniting warring clans. Under his leadership, a growing band of followers invaded Mecca in 630 A.D. and succeeded in taking it with hardly a fight. The city submitted to Muhammed and his warriors—accepting him as a prophet where he had previously been rejected.[15]

Now occupying Mecca, the Muslims began to wage war on the surrounding communities, forcing them to accept Islam as their only religion and Muhammed as their prophet.[16]

The Warrior

Though hailed by his followers as a "prophet of god," Muhammed was, in essence, a military leader—laying siege to towns, massacring the men, raping the women and enslaving their children. In most cases, Muhammed would confiscate the property of his victims—dividing it amongst himself and his men. On several occasions, he rejected offers of surrender from the besieged inhabitants and killed those whom he could have just as easily taken prisoner.[17]

Muhammed inspired his followers to battle, even when they did not feel that it was right to fight—threatening them with Hell if they did not and promising them slaves and spoils if they did.[18]

By the time of his unexpected death in 632 A.D., Muhammed had succeeded in uniting virtually the entire Arabian Peninsula under his rule. This rapidly expanding empire spread across North Africa, and also began to move north, conquering Jerusalem in the early 680s.

Islam After Muhammed

The Muslim armies were devoted solely to spreading the relig-ion of their one "true" god, Allah. Under Muhammed's successors, the *Caliphs*, they waged aggressive campaigns. The principle set in motion early on was that the civilian population of a town was to be destroyed if they attempted to defend themselves. In these cases, the men would be executed without reservation and the women and children taken as slaves.[19]

Modern Muslim apologists often claim that the Islamic warri-ors only attacked in "self-defense." This, of course, is not only an oxymoron but it is flatly contradicted by the accounts of Muslim historians and others, going back to the time of Muhammad.[20]

Oppression of Non-Believers, or "Dhimmitude"

Once established, the Islamic Empire worked actively to op-press nonbelievers—in particular Jews and Christians—strictly forbidding any proselytizing of Muslims on pain of death and threatening any Muslims who converted to another religion with the same.[21]

As part of a practice that would come to be known as "dhim-mitude," an extra tax (jizyah) was also placed on all who were for-tunate enough to be given the option of not converting to Islam.[22]

Additionally, Christians had no right to repair churches, or build new ones. Moreover, Muslims could confiscate and or de-stroy any church at their whim.[23]

Still other rules were put in place in order to subjugate non-Muslims. For instance, the houses of Christians or Jews were not allowed to overlook those of Muslims. Also, non-Muslims were forbidden to carry weapons or ride atop horses.[24]

A Long and Bloody Legacy

Under Muhammed and his successors, the *Caliphs*, the em-pires that formed beneath the banner of Islam—first the Arabic and then the Ottoman—ruled for nearly 1,300 years. Throughout the centuries, the bloody legacy of Muhammed would prove to be a source of constant dispute and confrontation for those living on the borders of lands controlled by Muslims. The violence that the Muslim armies would visit upon the people throughout the region is a testament to the teachings of a founder who condoned subjugation, rape, murder, and forced conversion as a means to spread his religion.

The Empire Collapses

Beginning in the 1600s, despite massive holdings of land and wealth, the Islamic Ottoman Empire began to slide into corruption and incompetence. By the time of the First World War, the empire was close to collapse and was ultimately defeated by the Allied forces.[25]

The Islamic Empire ended very much how it began—with a bloody onslaught directed at Christians. In what is widely acknowledged to be the first true genocide of the twentieth century, an estimated 1.5 million Christian Armenians were brutally slaughtered by Muslim Turks. The Armenians were uprooted from their homes under the pretext of "disloyalty" and forced to march hundreds of miles to concentration camps, where they would be indiscriminately massacred.[26]

…but Islam Continues

Although the Islamic Empire had collapsed, the religion of Islam, itself, did not collapse. Obviously, Islam continues to thrive and attract adherents from around the globe at an ever-increasing pace. In fact, one in five people currently practice the religion that was born fourteen centuries ago from Muhammed's encounter at the cave of Hira.

Conclusion

Most people, when asked about what drives the Middle East conflict, tend to cite the causes that we touched on in the previous chapter—such as the "contested religious sites" or the greatly misunderstood "Palestinian issue." However, as we have seen, the contempt that many Muslims harbor toward the Jews has much deeper roots than most realize. The ancient rivalry that was already thousands of years old by the time of Muhammed's first "revelation," was further ignited by the advent of Islam; indeed, one might liken the effect to that of throwing gasoline on a fire.

Today, owing to Islam, many Asian, Black or White Muslims, who, in fact, do not share the *Arab ancestry* and the correlating *ancient* hostility based on the loss of Esau's birth rite, have their own justification for hating the Jews: Muhammed hated the Jews.

Consequently, the religion of Islam has become yet another source of animosity and intolerance directed toward the descendants of Isaac and Jacob.

Due to the example set by Muhammed, Islam's most committed followers view daily life as a constant physical battle between Islamic society and the world of "nonbelievers." The principles that Muhammed established form the basis of the campaign of terror that is being waged against the West Today.

As Indonesian cleric, Abu Bakar Bashir, recently put it, *"If the West wants to have peace, then they have to accept Islamic rule."*

PART II

What Makes Islam "Islam?"

The police lineup is a time-honored method of identifying the perpetrator of a crime. Though, in order to confidently pick the suspect out of a crowd, one must have an accurate and trustworthy description of whom they are looking for. Such is the case in identifying the end-times "*beast*" of the Bible.

The premise of this book is based on the notion that Islam, as a religious and political ideology, is clearly recognizable in the Scriptures as the Beast that will rise to power in the last days. Yet, in order to confirm our suspicions, we must first get to know the "suspect."

Islam is unique among the world religions, today, in that it also serves as an all-encompassing governing system. For those living within Muslim societies, religion pervades every aspect of life—from law, to government, to personal behavior.

Thus, in the following four chapters, we are going to explore the unique elements that form the basis of Islam. In doing so, we will become fully prepared to identify the Beast—beyond the shadow of a doubt.

We begin our advanced study of Islam with an introduction to a book that is no doubt a best seller in many parts of the world.

THREE

May 14, 2005: At Least nine people were killed yesterday as a wave of anti-American demonstrations swept the Islamic world from the Gaza Strip to the Java Sea, sparked by a single paragraph in a magazine alleging that US military interrogators had desecrated the Koran. As Washington scrambled to calm the outrage, Condoleezza Rice, the US Secretary of State, promised an inquiry and punishment for any proven offenders. But at Friday prayers in the Muslim world many preachers demanded vengeance and afterwards thousands took to the streets, burning American flags.

—Catherine Philp, Timesonline

The Koran

T he Koran, or *Quran*, is known as the "holy book" of Islam. According to Muslims, it is the "most sacred" of all the religious texts. Muslims view the Koran as the actual "words of Allah," as spoken through the heart, mind, and lips of the prophet Muhammed—thereby claiming it to be the "last and final word" from god. In this sense, the Koran essentially serves as the *Bible* of Islam.

The Delivery of Revelation

As detailed previously, Muslim traditions hold that in the year 610 A.D., the angel Gabriel began appearing to Muhammed in order to deliver divine revelations from Allah. In these purported encounters, which would continue throughout his life, Muhammed would often claim to see the angel—other times he would only hear him—and at others, it is said that he heard "the sound of a bell" through which the words of the angel would come.[1]

The Earliest Recordings

Since Muhammed was not able to read or write, his companions recorded what he said. These recitations were copied onto a variety of materials, including papyrus, flat stones, palm leaves, pieces of leather, and wooden boards. The writings were compiled into a book (the Koran) some time after Muhammed's death.[2]

Committed to Memory

In addition to being written down, many of Muhammed's sayings were simply committed to memory by his followers and then passed down to the succeeding generations. This began a tradition in which memorization of the Koran would become a highly revered pursuit among Muslims.

In fact, to this day, there is no higher goal in Muslim life than to become a "human repository" of the holy book. One of the most prized honors in Islamic society is to reach the level of *hafiz*, or "one who has committed the entire scripture to memory."

Today, any Iranian citizen who accomplishes this feat receives an automatic university degree. It could therefore be said that the Koran is the very backbone of Muslim education.[3]

The Hallmarks of a Divine Work?

The Koran is divided into one hundred and fourteen chapters, called "Surahs," and is roughly the same size as the New Testament. Many have noted that the arrangement of the Koran is not chronological, or thematic, and that the subjects tend to be disjointed and shifting. Muslims are aware of this and consider it to be an indication of the "divine order" of the work.[4]

Scholars note that throughout the history of the Koran there have been numerous revisions, corrections, and alterations made to the text—though the present-day version cannot be checked for validity against an original, since none exist.[5]

Similarities to the Bible?

The Koran contains many of the same figures that we find in the Bible, including Abraham, David, Moses and Jesus. Moreover, the Islamic holy book continually references the stories of Moses and Abraham. Detractors of the Koran say that this is simply due to the fact that Muhammed was taking older religious stories from the Christian and Jewish faiths and incorporating them into his teachings—this, in an attempt to gain credibility among those whom he wished to convert.

Nonetheless, despite some superficial resemblances, the holy book of Islam offers a radical departure from the biblical stories and teachings. For instance, the Koran denies the deity of Jesus, insisting that He was not the Son of God, but only the *"son of Mary."* Another example is the story of Noah's Ark. According to the Bible, there were eight people on the Ark, and all of them survived the flood. The Koran, however, does not mention the number of souls on board the Ark, but does claim that one of Noah's sons was drowned. The account found in the Koran also questions whether Noah's wife survived. Curiously, there is also no mention of the *rainbow*, or of its significance, which is, of course, an integral part of the biblical version of the story.[6]

Muslims acknowledge the differences between the Koran and the Bible, considering them to be proof that the Bible has been corrupted by the Jews and Christians. According to Muslims, it is because of this corruption that the Bible cannot be trusted; thus, the Koran is the only source of "the truth."

The Other Sacred Islamic Writings

While the Koran is the most well-known of the Islamic writings, it is not the only source of sacred or inspired tradition within Islam. The Sunna, or *well-trodden path*, references the actions that Muhammed had taken in life—as well as the things he condoned or condemned.

To be sure, Muslims view Muhammed as being the archetype of the perfect human being; consequently, whatever he said or did in life becomes the ideal after which any dedicated Muslim should model his own behavior.

The source material for the Sunna is taken from two different types of Islamic literature: The *Hadith* (written record of Muhammed's sayings) and the *Sirat* (biography literature of Muhammed's life).

It could be said that the Sunna actually *interprets* the Koran, and without it the Koran cannot be properly understood. In this way, the Koran and the Sunna combine to form the foundation of the beliefs and practices of all Muslims.[7]

Concealing the True Message of the Koran

In today's often politically correct world, many Muslims will deny the fact that the Koran commands them to do harm to others—insisting that the supposed "violent verses" are "taken out of context" or are "abrogated" (cancelled out) by others. Most often in the public arena, Muslims will claim that these "questionable" verses are not to be taken as the "last word" of the prophet.

These assertions are a perfect example of *Taqiyya*, or *Kithman*—both of which are forms of deception in which some information is held back.[8] According to Islamic doctrine, this practice is not the same as telling a lie, but is likened to an innocent misrepresentation that the public will most likely accept without questioning. For the Muslim, it is often times a matter of simply avoiding the facts that contradict what he is saying.

To a greater extent, these methods of deception can be taken as far as denying or concealing one's own faith or religious convictions. This is considered to be acceptable among Muslims if it serves the greater purpose of Islam or if one is in imminent danger because of his beliefs.

The following example illustrates how a Koranic verse might be creatively edited in order to obscure the true message:

On that account: We ordained for the Children of Israel that if anyone slew a person <u>unless it be for murder or for spreading mischief (corruption) in the land</u> it would be as if he slew the whole people: and if anyone saved a life it would be as if he saved the life of the whole people. <u>Then there came to them Our apostles with clear Signs yet even after that many of them (Jews) continued to commit excesses in the land.</u>

—Surah 5:32

It is the underlined portions of the above passage that many Muslim apologists revise, or selectively omit. This is the part of the verse that, in effect, cancels out the other parts—allowing for the *slaying* of the *"Children of Israel,"* as many of them continue to *"commit excesses in the land."* Below, we have the edited verse that would most likely be quoted in public:

> If anyone slew a person…it would be as if he slew the whole people: and if anyone saved a life it would be as if he saved the life of the whole people.

The edited verse, removed from its true context within the Koran, is much more suited for public consumption. Undoubtedly, the use of Taqiyya and Kithman, in conjunction with today's general atmosphere of political correctness and multiculturalism, has proven to be a very powerful weapon in the advancement of Islam.

Muhammed's Later Revelations: Verses of Violence

Muhammed's revelations can be broken into two distinct periods: the Meccan and the Medinian. Generally, it is within the later (Medinian) revelations, after Muhammed had been rejected by the Jews and Christians, that we find an increasing call for violence and cruelty. The well-known Surah 9 is a good example of this:

> "When the sacred forbidden months for fighting are past, fight and kill the disbelievers wherever you find them, take them captive, torture them, and lie in wait and ambush them using every stratagem of war."
> —Surah 9:5

This verse is cited more than any other as abrogating less aggressive Koranic passages. It is said to have cancelled out no fewer than one hundred and twenty-four verses of the Koran. In fact, it is the violent verses, such as this one, that most often cancel out the earlier "religion of peace" variety.

By many accounts, the Koran contains as many as one hundred

and nine verses that call Muslims to war with nonbelievers.[9] Some are quite graphic, with commands to chop off heads and fingers, and to kill "infidels" wherever they may be found. Muslims who do not join in the fight are called "hypocrites" and warned that Allah will send them to Hell if they do not battle the enemy alongside their fellow Muslims.

To get a better sense of the violent and hateful tone that is often set in the Koran, we note a sampling of the verses that call on Muslims to *"fight"* for the cause of Allah. The first (5:33) is tied to verse 5:32, which was discussed earlier in regard to deception (Taqiyya and Kithman) within Islam. The two combine to create a single message in which Muhammad makes it very clear that those who *"perpetuate mischief"* (Jews, Christians, pagans and all non-Muslims) are to be killed:

> "The punishment for those who wage war against Allah and His Prophet and perpetrate mischief (reject Islam or oppose its goals) in the land, is to murder them, to hang them, to mutilate them, or banish them. Such is their disgrace. They will not escape the fire, suffering constantly."
> —Surah 5:33

> "Fighting is enjoined on you, and it is an object of dislike to you; and it may be that you dislike a thing while it is good for you, and it may be that you love a thing while it is evil for you, and Allah knows, while you do not know."
> —Surah 2:216

> "But you (Jews) went back on your word and were lost losers. So become apes, despised and hated. We made an example out of you."
> —Surah 2:64

> "Fight those who believe not in Allah nor the Last Day nor hold that forbidden which hath been forbidden by Al-

lah and His apostle nor acknowledge the religion of truth (even if they are) of the People of the Book until they pay the Jizya (tax on nonbelievers) with willing submission and feel themselves subdued."

—Surah 9:29

"He punished them by putting hypocrisy in their hearts until the Day whereon they shall meet Him, because they lied to Allah and failed to perform as promised. Allah knows their secrets. Those who slander and taunt the believers who pay the zakat (for Allah's Cause) voluntarily and throw ridicule on them, scoffing, Allah will throw back their taunts, and they shall have a painful doom. Whether you ask for their forgiveness or not, (their sin is unforgivable). If you ask seventy times for their forgiveness Allah will not forgive them."

—Surah 9:77

A recurring theme in the Koran appears to be that those who deny Islam should be punished to the point of submission or death. With threats of *"disgrace," "suffering,"* and *"painful doom,"* the words of Allah condemn Christians and Jews.

Indeed, the Koran is unique from all other religious writings, in that it has adopted as one of its fundamental precepts the destruction of those who worship the God of the Bible. This fact, perhaps, reveals much about the true spiritual origins of the book itself.

Conclusion

We conclude our brief introduction to the Koran and the other sacred Islamic writings by citing an example from the Hadith, which details the *conversion method* that is prescribed for Muslims: *"Allah's apostle said, I have been ordered to fight with the people till they say, 'None has the right to be worshipped but Allah'" (Bukhari 4:52:196).*

In contrast to the commands to forcefully advance Islam, the Bible teaches that God's Word is to be spread in peace. For instance, while the Scriptures certainly do call on Christians to "*go and make disciples of all nations*" *(Matthew 28:19)*, this is to be done "*with gentleness and respect*" *(1 Peter 3:15)*, as Christians do not use "*the weapons of the world*" *(2 Corinthians 10:3-5)* to preach the Gospel.

Surely, to force one's religion on anyone, or to "*fight*" those who choose to deny a particular faith, would seem to be in direct opposition to the God given gift of free will.

FOUR

And they had a king over them, which is the angel of the bottomless pit, whose name in the Hebrew tongue is Abaddon, but in the Greek tongue hath his name Apollyon.

—Revelation 9:11

Who is Allah?

Recently, a Roman Catholic Bishop from the Netherlands suggested that Christians start calling God "Allah," because he believes that it would promote harmony between Christians and Muslims. Appearing on Dutch television, he said, *"Allah is a very beautiful word for God. Shouldn't we all say that from now on we will name God Allah? What does God care what we call him?"*[1]

As demonstrated by our Catholic Bishop friend, many today are grossly misinformed, assuming that Allah is simply another name for the God that Christians and Jews worship.

It appears that even our own President Bush—who is charged with heading up the war on radical Islam—is not immune to misunderstanding on the matter. This is evidenced in an October 2007 White House interview in which he was quoted as saying, *"Well, first of all, I believe in an almighty God, and I believe that all the world, whether they be Muslim, Christian, or any other religion, prays to the same God. That's what I believe."*[2]

While the President's statement is obviously well intentioned, it could not be further from the truth.

As will be highlighted throughout this book, the majority of those living in the West are generally uninformed with respect to the facts surrounding the world's second largest religion. It should therefore come as no surprise that most do not have the foggiest idea as to the origins of Allah, the god to whom observant Muslims bow in prayer to five times each day.

Be that as it may, for those willing to do a little research, the answers are not far from reach.

The Archaeological Origins of Allah

Many scholars agree that Allah, far from being the biblical God of Abraham, Isaac and Jacob, was actually the name attributed to the pre-Islamic pagan moon-god. During the last two centuries, prominent archaeologists have unearthed thousands of inscriptions which indicate that the dominant religion of Arabia during Muhammed's day was based on worship of this moon-god.

Moreover, history tells us that for generations before Muhammed was born, the Arabs worshipped some three hundred and sixty pagan gods that were housed at a stone temple in Mecca, known as the "Kaaba." The pre-Islamic Arabs worshipped the moon-god by bowing in prayer toward Mecca several times each day. They would make a pilgrimage to Mecca, walk around the Kaaba seven times and "throw stones at the devil." The ancients would also fast for one month, which began with the appearance of the crescent moon and ended when the crescent moon reappeared. These same pagan rites form the core of Islam today.[3]

Historians note that when Muhammed chose a name for his god, he consciously adopted the name of the chief deity within the Arabian pantheon (Allah), making it the *only* god. In doing so, he was simply mimicking the other monotheistic faiths (Judaism and Christianity) by instituting the concept of one all-powerful deity.

Considering the pagan origins of Allah, it makes perfect sense that the ancient symbol of the moon-god, the crescent moon, is, today, the official symbol of Islam; it appears on the flags of Muslim countries, as well as the tops of mosques and minarets everywhere.

Allah's Nature Revealed

The Bible and the Koran each present ideas about the character of God that are, in essence, diametrically opposed to each other—so much so that any reasonable observer would have to conclude that each book refers to a distinct deity. For instance, the Koran states unequivocally that Allah is an *unknowable* and non-personal being. In contrast, the God of the Bible allows Himself to be known, and actually desires personal fellowship with humankind. The Scriptures clearly acknowledge that Abraham—the same Abraham whom Muslims say they venerate—was a friend of God.

We find further disparity between the Christian and Muslim gods in that there is no "law of righteousness" in the being of Allah. He does as he pleases and, at his whim, guides some men aright and others astray. Similarly, it is a widely held belief among Muslims that Allah created some men and spirits specifically for the purpose of sending them to Hell.[4]

The Koran generally portrays Allah as a vindictive deity, who hates sinners and desires to afflict them. He appears to have no affection for any creature. Love is conditional and reserved for those who believe and do good works. Conversely, the Bible tells us that the very essence of God is love: *Whoever does not love does not know God, because God is love (1 John 4:8).*

The Ninety-Nine Beautiful Names of God

Islam teaches that there are ninety-nine names for god.[5] The rationale being that Allah is bigger than one name—in fact, so incomprehensible that it is hard to put a frame around the measure of his divinity.

The names also serve as reminders of the various aspects of god; for instance, the *Merciful*, the *Compassionate*, and the *Unfathomable*. They are further used as a tool by Muslims to get to know their creator more completely, as god has not revealed himself in the religion of Islam.

Without a doubt, many Muslims believe that by trying to emulate the ninety-nine beautiful names of god, they are striving to become better people.

Yet, for all of the seemingly positive aspects of this Muslim convention, it seems that there is also a darker side. Interestingly, not all of the ninety-nine names allude to attributes that most Christians or Jews would normally ascribe to a benevolent God.

The following list highlights some of the less celebrated aspects of Allah, the god of Islam:

Al-Jabbar: *the Oppressor*, the All Compelling, who compensates lacks of others

Al-Mutakabbir: *the Haughty,* the Majestic, the Lord

Al-Qabid: *the Contractor, the Restrainer*, the Recipient

Al-Khafid: *the Abaser, the Humbler*, the Pleaser

Al-Mumeet: *the Bringer of Death, the Death Giver*

Al-Batin: *the Hidden*, the Interior, the Veiled

Al-Muzil: the *Abaser, the Subduer*

Al-Muntaqim: *the Avenger*

Ad-Daarr: the *Distresser, the Afflictor, the Bringer of Adversity*

For anyone who has ever opened a Bible, it goes without saying that these traits are not among those typically associated with the Judeo-Christian God. If truth be told, from a Christian perspective, many of the qualities that Muslims attribute to Allah would be recognized as those more commonly linked to a well-known fallen angel, who is, of course, in opposition to God.

For example, it is interesting to note that "Al-Jabbar" (the Oppressor) was chosen as one of Allah's names. In the Old Testament (Isaiah 14), the title of *"the oppressor"* is used to refer to the Antichrist.

Some of the other ninety-nine names suggest traits that are anything but godly, such as "Al-Mutakabbir" (the Haughty). Consulting a thesaurus, we find that "haughty" is a word used to describe one who is *detached, distant, scornful, disdainful, or conceited.*

Another name that is ascribed to Allah is "Al-Muzil" (the Abaser). To "abase" is to *belittle, degrade, demean, humiliate, or dishonor.*

Remarkably, these names, along with the others, are well known within the Islamic world and are frequently displayed in homes, places of worship, and on the dorm room walls of Muslim students everywhere.

Conclusion

In closing this chapter, we make note of what is possibly the most glaring distinction that can be drawn between the god of Islam and the God of the Bible: The New Testament teaches that God so loved mankind that He sent His only Son to earth to pay the debt for humanity's sins. Consequently, salvation is available for free to anyone who accepts Jesus Christ as their personal Savior. Islam, of course, denies that Christ was the Son of God or that He died in order to save humanity. Therefore, Allah does not provide any way for man to be reconciled to god—leaving many Muslims uncertain of their ultimate destiny.

From what we have learned about the god of Islam, it is clear that although Muslims claim to worship the "God of Abraham," Allah should in no way be confused with the God of the Torah and the New Testament. In truth, he could not be more contradictory in nature.

FIVE

"Everything you have in the West is wrong. We should be in charge over you. If Sharia law prevailed, it would change everything."

—Khalid Kelly: an Irish Muslim convert

Islamic Law

S trict Islamic Law, or *Sharia*, is the code of law based on the Koran. Sharia means *the way*, or *the path*, and for those living within a legal system based on Muslim principles of equity, it provides the framework which regulates many aspects of both public and private life—including politics, economics, business, family, and social issues.[1]

Islamic Law is not like "law" as most of us know it in the West. As far as Muslims are concerned, there is no separation between church and state. Within Islam, religion and government are profoundly intertwined, as worship of Allah influences every aspect of life. For instance, Islamic schools teach children primarily from the Koran, while, in contrast, Western society has been working diligently toward the removal of every vestige of God and spirituality from classrooms—as well as most other aspects of public life.

Is Sharia as Brutal as Some Would Have You Believe?

For many, the term Sharia conjures images of a brutal and inhumane legal system, characterized by amputations, beheadings, and stonings. Obviously, these types of punishments would be considered excessive or barbaric by Western standards. Yet, they are a reality for many of those living under Sharia in Muslim countries.

To gain a sense of the penalties required under Sharia Law, we note some examples from *Reliance of the Traveller: A Classic Manual of Islamic Sacred Law* (Shafi'i School):

pg. 613 "THE PENALTY FOR THEFT.... A person's

right hand is amputated, whether he is a Muslim, non-Muslim subject of the Islamic state, or someone who has left Islam...."

pg. 616 "THE PENALTY FOR HIGHWAY ROBBERY.... If he steals the equivalent of 1.058 grams of gold..., both his right hand and left foot are amputated.... If the highwayman robs and kills, he is killed and then left crucified for three days."

pg. 610 "THE PENALTY FOR FORNICATION OR SODOMY.... If the offender is someone with the capacity to remain chaste, then he or she is stoned to death...."

pg. 595 "APOSTASY FROM ISLAM (RIDDA).... When a person who has reached puberty and is sane voluntarily apostatizes from Islam, he deserves to be killed."

pg. 617 "THE PENALTY FOR DRINKING.... The penalty for drinking is to be scourged forty stripes, with hands, sandals, and ends of clothes. It may be administered with a whip, but if the offender dies, an indemnity... is due... for his death." [This penalty applies only to Muslims.]

Muslim apologists downplay the association of these seemingly draconian punishments with Sharia, as though such notions could only come from "ignorance." They insist that although these measures are certainly a "part" of Sharia, they are rarely carried out today—further arguing that there is a strictly enforced "list of qualifiers," which specifies who can and who cannot be punished.

In spite of the claims of these apologists, however, there is ample evidence that these barbaric practices are still very much alive. In fact, Aid organizations, such as the Red Cross, have found it necessary to have a policy in place that addresses whether or not to assist with amputations meted out as punishment in Muslim countries. There are also reports of stonings that are being carried out by the legal system in Nigeria, Iran and elsewhere.[2]

Sex Crimes?

Sex outside of marriage is often considered to be part of normal daily life for many in the West; yet, in some Muslim countries, people are essentially being condemned to death for this very offense.

The accounts listed below describe actual sentences that have been carried out under Sharia for convictions of *"non-marital sex."* Gathered by the Ontario Consultants on Religious Tolerance, these excerpts illustrate how severe Sharia can be:

1996-NOV: Afghanistan: Under the previous Taliban regime, a woman, Nurbibi, 40, and a man, Turylai, 38, were stoned to death in a public assembly using palm-sized stones. They were found guilty of non-marital sex. Turylai was dead within ten minutes, but Nurbibi had to be finished off by dropping a large rock on her head. Mr. Wali, head of the Office for the Propagation of Virtue and the Prohibition of Vice expressed satisfaction with the execution: *"...I am very happy, because it means that the rule of Islam is being implemented."*[3]

2000-NOV: Nigeria: Attine Tanko, 18, is found guilty of having pre-marital sex out of wedlock. She was discovered to be pregnant. Her sentence of 100 lashes was deferred for up to two years after the birth, so that she could breastfeed her baby. Her boyfriend, 23, was flogged 100 times and given jail time.[4]

2002-JUN: Nigeria: A Sharia court convicted a man, Yunusa Rafin Chiwaya, of adultery in the northern state of Bauchi, and *sentenced him to be stoned to death.* He had confessed to engaging in sexual activities with his neighbor's wife, and had declined multiple opportunities to withdraw his confession. The woman in the case was cleared after she swore on the Qur'an that she had been hypnotized before she left home with Chiwaya.[5]

Though most would agree that these punishments are beyond extreme—particularly for what is, in essence, a victimless crime— there are those who would not take issue with this type of enforcement, as long as it is kept within the confines of Islamic society. The rationalization being that if Muslims want to impose this type of law because it reflects their religious and cultural beliefs, then what right does Western society have to protest?

In some respects, this point is a valid one. Yet, the problem that the West is now facing appears to be that of keeping Islamic Law restricted solely to Muslim nations. The reality is that in recent years, the notion of Sharia Law *beyond* the borders of Islamic countries has been gaining momentum. For instance, there have already been petitions for Sharia to be adopted for the Muslim community within numerous European and Western nations that have sizeable Muslim populations.

As has been demonstrated in non-Muslim countries throughout the world, once the Islamic community grows in size and becomes a majority—or has the power to influence elections—it is no longer satisfied to impose Sharia exclusively on Muslims but will lobby for Islamic law to be implemented for all citizens. The ultimate aim of Islam is, of course, to dominate—meaning that *all* must eventually submit to the Law of the Koran.

The Call for Sharia in Europe

In Europe, many young Muslims are defying the British culture and increasingly asking for Sharia Law to be adopted. Much of the call for the enforcement of Islamic ideals is considered by observers to be a predictable reaction on the part of Muslims to life in the West—specifically citing exposure to the darker side of what Muslims perceive to be *Western* values, such as repeated drunkenness and fighting among young people in the streets or outside of public bars.

The fact is that many Muslims simply do not wish to live under Western law and Western rule, even when living in Western societies. According to polls in the sixteen to twenty-four age group, forty percent of British Muslims would prefer to live under Sharia Law, which, again, includes such punishments as beheading and stoning.[6]

While many are startled to learn that the idea of Sharia Law is gaining popularity in Europe, one finds some comfort in the fact that this burgeoning outgrowth of Islamic society has not taken root near the borders of America; at least, that was, until recently.

Sharia Next Door

Canada is host to a thriving Muslim population centered in Ontario. In 2004, to the dismay of many—namely some prominent women's rights groups—a report by Ontario's former Attorney General, Marian Boyd, recommended the use of Islamic Law to settle civil issues, such as divorce and child custody.[7] If this proposal were to be implemented, two Muslims involved in a dispute over property, a business contract, or a marriage, would take the problem to a Muslim arbitrator and reach an agreement based on *Sharia principles*.

While many believe that this *modified* version of Sharia would be harmless enough, the concern expressed by citizens is that the terms of these agreements might eventually wind up being overseen and imposed by Canadian courts. Thus, Canadian police and courts would become the enforcers of Islamic Law on Canadian citizens!

Fortunately, soon after Boyd's recommendations, protests sprang up across Canada and numerous cities around the globe, including

Amsterdam, Dusseldorf, Stockholm, London, and Paris.

Later, in a 2005 decision, Ontario Premier, Dalton McGuinty, ruled against the move, maintaining that there should be "one law for all Ontarians," and also citing concerns that religious courts would threaten the "common ground" of Canadian citizens.[8]

Sharia in Our Future?

While, ultimately, common sense prevailed and the recommendation put forth by Boyd was not implemented, it is, perhaps, very telling that the idea was proposed to begin with. Needless to say, many commentators find it alarming that Sharia is beginning to rear its head just north of the U.S. border.

As some have noted, the proposed adoption of centuries-old religious laws within the borders of a Western country is simply the result of multiculturalism and tolerance gone out of control. It is a predictable consequence of a culture that wishes to appease its newest citizens, even to the detriment of its own established culture and values.

While we in the United States will most likely not be living under Sharia Law any time soon, we should nevertheless find what is happening in Europe, Canada, and many other parts of the world, unnerving.

As for now, it appears as though the first seeds of Sharia have already been sown in the West. Will Islamic Law eventually take root and spread throughout the world? Only time and a growing Muslim population will tell.

SIX

And the ten horns which thou sawest are ten kings, which have received no kingdom as yet; but receive power as kings one hour with the beast.

—Revelation 17:12

The Caliphate

U nless you follow events in the Middle East very closely, or have studied the history of the former Islamic Empire, the term *Caliphate* is likely one that you are not familiar with. It is, however, a term that is being brought ever increasingly into the mainstream, even to the extent of being addressed in some of President Bush's speeches—and justifiably so.

In light of today's global political climate, the subject of the Caliphate is one that deserves our utmost consideration—this, in order to get a sense of how the Muslim world was once ruled and, also, to help us envision what the future may hold, given what the Bible forecasts toward the end of the age.

Indeed, as some far-sighted Middle East commentators have suggested, it is quite possible that the Caliphate may soon become a term that virtually everyone is acquainted with.

A Leader for all Muslims

The Caliphate was the governing authority that ruled the Islamic Empire, in various forms, from the time just after Muhammed's death, in the year 632 A.D., until 1924. The Caliphate or *Khalifate*, system features a singular leader, known as the "Caliph" or "Commander of the Faithful," who heads worldwide Islam.[1] His authority is beyond dispute within the Islamic world, and his decisions are completely binding on all Muslims.

Fulfilling a dual role, the Caliph serves not only as the spiritual leader but as the *political* head of Islam. He leads Muslims in all new matters and is considered to be the ultimate arbiter and enforcer of Sharia. The Caliph also administers the government and conducts relations with other states, which includes full authority and oversight over all military operations.

The First Caliph

The appointment of the first Caliph came about as a corollary of Muhammed's death. The Muslim world was in need of a ruler to fill the prophet's shoes and carry the torch of Islam. And so, a long-time friend, Abu Bakr, was selected as Muhammed's successor. He would be the first in a long line of Caliphs who would assume the role of leader for all Muslims.[2]

The selection of Abu Bakr as Caliph was a decision that sparked immediate controversy within the Muslim community and would prove to have long-lasting consequences. At the time, another Muslim faction preferred that someone from the immediate family (specifically Muhammed's son-in-law) fill the role; though, eventually, they would abandon their position—submitting to the group who favored Bakr.[3]

While this difference of opinion among the Muslim factions may seem like a minor political dilemma to most in the West, the question of "who should be the Caliph," was, and still is, the greatest dividing issue within Islam. This dispute is, in fact, the defining criteria of Shiites and Sunnis.[4]

Today, many are shocked to learn that the seemingly unending strife between the two major branches of Islam—as evidenced in the ongoing battle between the Shiites and Sunnis in Iraq—can be traced back to this initial disagreement, which took place nearly 1,400 years ago.

An Enormous Empire

The Caliphate grew rapidly in geographic terms. By the eighth century—only one hundred years after the death of Muhammed—the authority of the Caliphs had expanded westward across North Africa and into what is now Spain and Portugal, also spreading eastward through Persia and, ultimately, to the region that we know as Pakistan.

The massive expanse of land that was governed under the Islamic Empire made it one of the largest unitary states in the history of West Eurasia—extending its entire breadth. It was also one of the few states in history to ever extend direct rule over three continents: Africa, Europe, and Asia.[5]

An Enduring Empire

In addition to the immense geographic holdings that fell under the rule of the Caliphate, scholars note that the historical timeline of the Islamic Empire was also far-reaching: Between the Arabic and Ottoman Empires, the Caliphs ruled for a period of nearly 1,300 years.

Notably, from an overall perspective, ninety-four percent of Islamic history has taken place under the governance of a Caliphate; or, to frame it otherwise, of the nearly 1,400 years that the religion of Islam has existed, Muslims have only been without a singular leader, or *Caliph*, for the relatively short period of eighty-four years.

The Fall of the Caliphate

The Caliphate system was abolished in 1924, with the defeat of the Islamic Ottoman Empire. The first President of the Turkish Republic, Gazi Mustafa Kemal Ataturk, as part of his reforms, annulled the institution of "one leader for all Muslims," and the governing powers of the Caliph were transferred to the newly formed Turkish Parliament.[6]

The loss of the Caliph may be the single most pivotal event in modern Islam. It was considered to be a humiliating blow to Muslims at the time and remains as a thorn in the side of many to this very day. This is evidenced in a videotaped statement released after 9/11, in which Osama bin Laden celebrated the fact that the United States was finally tasting the kind of *"humiliation and dis-*

grace" that the Muslim community has felt "*for more than eighty years.*"

Experts agree that by using the figure of exactly eighty years, bin Laden was almost certainly referring to the fall of the Caliphate in 1924.[7]

To be sure, bin Laden and many other like-minded Islamists see the demise of the Caliphate as the event that paved the way for the downturn within the Islamic community as a whole. Most would agree that it is this general lack of unity that has kept Muslim nations from exercising the type of political, economic, and military authority that the Islamic Empire had once enjoyed.

Gone, but not Forgotten

Historically a subject of intense conflict and rivalry among Muslim rulers, the Caliphate system has lain dormant and largely unclaimed since the 1920s. However, in recent years, there has been a steadily increasing call for Muslims to, once again, unite under a singular ruler. Today, many Muslim fundamentalist groups agree that the re-establishment of the Caliphate is a necessary step in the advancement of Islamic influence around the globe. In fact, Osama bin Laden and his fellow jihadists have repeatedly declared that the "ultimate objective" of their struggle is to "restore the Islamic Caliphate."[8]

What Muslims Are Saying

The following collection of quotes comes from a broad range of Muslim leaders and activists. These statements underscore the sense of determination harbored among many in the Muslim world with regard to the restoration of the Caliphate:

"Next week marks the 83rd anniversary of the collapse of caliphate, that unprecedented tragedy in the history of mankind where the Islamic way of life came to a halt, a

*halt that we believe is only temporary one. We look for-
ward to the rising new dawn of Islam."*[9]

  —Abu Shaker, an activist from Hizb ut-Tahrir
  in Lebanon.

*"As long as there are infidels and enemies of God in His
kingdom, this movement will continue its jihad. Today,
the nation of Muhammad has everything but an Islamic
caliphate. We have clerics, mujahideen, and fedayeen, but
not a caliphate. One of the most important goals of the Islamic movement of Uzbekistan is to establish an Islamic
caliphate at any price."*[10]

  —Muhammad Taher Al-Farouq, leader of the
  Islamic Movement of Uzbekistan

*"Our ultimate goal is, of course, after the liberation of
Palestine, the establishment of the Islamic state where
everybody, and I am emphasizing on everybody, will live
in full honor and respect of its rights as those are guaran-
teed in our Quran,"…"The new Islamic state is the big
state for all Muslims. The state that will be ruled by
Sharia laws through a Calipha and will replace all those
corrupted and artificial states which were founded by the
West in order to hurt, to beat and to divide the unity of Islam and the Muslims."*[11]

  —Abu Muhammad, Palestinian terrorist and
  Senior member of the Dugmash clan.

The New Caliphate: It's not Just for Extremists

In an October 2001 article, Newsday's Middle East Bureau
Chief, Mohamad Bazzi, wrote: *"By launching a 'holy war' against
the United States, Osama bin Laden would like a return to the
glory days of the Muslim empire."*

Considering that Bazzi is referring to the leader of a foremost terrorist group, his observation may not come as much of a shock. Yet, many are surprised to learn that the more radical organizations, such as al-Qaeda, are not alone in favoring the return of the Caliphate. The reality is that a number of the supposedly non-violent Islamic groups, such as the pan-Islamic Hizb ut-Tahrir (Party of Liberation), champion the same cause.

A Show of Support

In August of 2007, a massive demonstration of support was widely covered in the Arab media. This gathering was touted as the "largest international conference gathering" of its type. More than ninety thousand leaders and supporters of Hizb ut-Tahrir gathered in Indonesia to call for the revival of the Caliphate; the goal being to unite all Muslims under Sharia Law in Indonesia, as well as the rest of the Muslim world.[12]

Punctuated by chants of "Allahu Akbar" (god is great) from the massive crowd at the Gelora Bung Karno Stadium in Jakarta, speaker after speaker petitioned for the return of the Caliphate system—appealing for unity among the Muslims who are now divided into fifty nations.[13]

What Does the Average Muslim on the Street Think?

Obviously, the notion of a revived Caliphate has garnered widespread support among the full range of Muslim organizations, but it seems that the enthusiasm does not end there. The idea has also found favor with the average Muslim on the street. For instance, more than two-thirds of people recently polled in four Muslim nations say that they support the idea of unifying all Muslim countries into a single Islamic state, or Caliphate.[14]

Could it Really Happen?

Although the call for a new Caliphate is obviously gaining momentum, there are those who believe that the re-establishment of this type of governing system may be more easily said than done. Aside from the obvious hindrances, such as differing beliefs and practices among various Muslim factions, these skeptics point to several obstacles that seem to stand in the way of a united Muslim world; one, of course, being the tight restrictions that are placed on political activity in many Muslim nations.

Further still, some Islamic groups cite a "lack of spirituality," along with a decline in "religious observance"—claiming that the Caliphate cannot be successfully revived until these deficiencies are addressed.

Nevertheless, some experts speculate that these issues may simply be negated by the prevalent driving force for unity against the West.[15]

The Consequences of a New Caliphate

The type of accord to be gained from a Caliphate-based government has not existed in the Muslim world for nearly a century. The implications of such a government would be staggering, in that the Middle East would no longer consist mostly of separate Muslim states—each vying for power and promoting its own political agenda.

An Islamic Caliphate would be an immense, extremely wealthy, and potentially nuclear armed empire that is hostile toward the West. In essence, all Muslims and their available resources would be combined in working toward a commonly held goal: the elimination of the "Great Satan" (United States) and the "Little Satan" (Israel). Indeed, many Muslims see the U.S. and Israel as the primary obstacles that stand in the way of establishing Islam as the only religion.

In Recent News

To get a better sense of what a new Caliphate, or Islamic Empire, might look like, we consider some excerpts taken from recently published articles and blogs. The observations made by these commentators underscore the fact that the proverbial "writing is on the wall." It appears as though this new appeal for Muslim unity is most definitely not a passing fad.

The call for a world-wide Caliphate - its official
Debbie Hamilton
Web source: Right Truth 3/06/06

From the Temple Mount in Jerusalem Sheikh Ismail Nawahda issued the call to restore the Moslem Khalifate, or, "Genuine Islamic Rule." The last caliphate was held by Ottoman Turkish sultans until it was abolished by Kemal Atatürk in 1924, after Turkey became a democratic republic. *Nawahda specifically called upon the Arabs of the Palestinian Authority to rise above their personal and party interests.*

A plan for the "Return of the Khalifate" was published secretly in 2002 by a group called "The Guiding Helper Foundation." The group explained that it wished to "give direction to the educated Muslim populace in its increasing interest in the establishment of Islam as a practical system of rule."

This past Friday, Feb. 24, however, the plan went public. Sheikh Nawahda called publicly for the renewal of the Islamic Khalifate, which would "unite all the Moslems in the world against the infidels."

The Khalifate system features a leader, known as a Khalif, who heads worldwide Islam. Assisted by a ten-man council, his decisions are totally binding on all Moslems.

The system by which the caliphate would be restored would

begin by establishing small groups all over the world. The infidels would have a "much harder task, if not impossible, if they are faced with a myriad of small groups of differing locations, ethnicities," etc. This method also "ensures that if one group...is found and cut off, other similar groups will remain undetected..."[16]

(emphasis mine)

Another...

The Caliphate is Coming
By Dr. Rachel Ehrenfeld
FrontPageMagazine.com 1/31/2006

To Mousa Abu Marzuk, Deputy Chief of Hamas' Political Bureau in Damascus, HAMAS' triumph is an important springboard towards the establishment of the Caliphate -- a global Islamic state, where life would be dictated by the Shari'a.

...The system's "obligations" institutionalize discrimination (dhimmitude) that targets Jews and Christians only. Others, such as Hindus, and Buddhists have a choice to convert or to be slaughtered. These regulations prohibit them from possessing arms, ringing church bells, testifying in courts, building and restoring houses of worship while restricting many other civil rights as well. Like Nazi regulations, *the Shari'a also requires non-Muslims to wear special, identifying clothes*. These key features of the Shari'a and Islamic ideology as called for by the MB and HAMAS, are political, not merely religious.

...The spiritual leader of Hamas, the late Ahmad Yassin said: "The 21st century is the century of Islam," and his successor Mahmoud Zahar says, "Israel will disappear and after it the US." With its recent victory, HAMAS seems to be closer to reaching this goal…

…Compare Hamas statements and its charter to those of al-Qaeda, Hizbullah and other Islamist organizations. All strive to establish a caliphate encircling the globe. Al-Qaeda says: "We will turn the White House and the British parliament into mosques." as documented by Jonathan Dahoah Halevi, director of Orient Research Group in Toronto.[17]

(emphasis mine)

Once more, what has attracted the attention of many Middle East observers, is the recurring theme that we see in these excerpts—specifically the fact that leaders of the various Islamic groups (namely HAMAS, al-Qaeda, and Hizbullah) are all calling on Muslims to look beyond their personal party agendas in the interest of unity within the Muslim world.

Also, the reference to *"dhimmitude"* should be of particular interest to all non-Muslims. As was detailed in chapter two, dhimmitude is an Islamic term for what essentially amounts to institutionalized discrimination. Again, this not so subtle form of bigotry was the standard practice under the Caliphs of the former Islamic Empire.

A striking example of dhimmitude is illustrated in the reference to non-Muslims being required to wear *"special identifying clothes."* Many believe that this practice originated with the Nazis, but history tells us that this tradition began in the lands of the early Islamic Caliphates. The practice of marking Jews and Christians was developed as a convenient way to identify who was, and who was not, a Muslim. This Islamic institution is what eventually led to the Nazi practice of requiring all Jews to don the yellow Star of David during World War Two.[18]

Having noted this "Caliphate related trivia," let us look at yet another excerpt, in which commentator, David J. Jonsson, highlights the growing—albeit slowly—awareness in the West, by including some remarks in a speech given by President Bush in September of 2006. The President's remarks are followed by Jonsson's own observations.

Caliphatism - Establishing the Kingdom of Allah
by David J. Jonsson
Globalpolitician.com 9/11/2006

The terrorists who attacked us on September the 11th, 2001, are men without conscience -- but they're not madmen. They kill in the name of a clear and focused ideology, a set of beliefs that are evil, but not insane. These al Qaeda terrorists and those who share their ideology are violent Sunni extremists. They're driven by a radical and perverted vision of Islam that rejects tolerance, crushes all dissent, and justifies the murder of innocent men, women and children in the pursuit of political power. They hope to establish a violent political utopia across the Middle East, which they call a "Caliphate" -- where all would be ruled according to their hateful ideology. Osama bin Laden has called the 9/11 attacks -- in his words -- "a great step towards the unity of Muslims and establishing the Righteous (Caliphate)."

This caliphate would be a totalitarian Islamic empire encompassing all current and former Muslim lands, stretching from Europe to North Africa, the Middle East, and Southeast Asia. We know this because al Qaeda has told us. About two months ago, the terrorist Zawahiri - he's al Qaeda's second in command -- declared that al Qaeda intends to impose its rule in every land that was a home for Islam, from Spain (Andalusia) to Iraq. He went on to say, "The whole world is an open field for us."

(end president's speech)

Begin David J. Jonsson's commentary…

…Islam's ultimate goal is the creation of "one world without borders under Islamic rule," a totalitarian economic political theocracy based on Islamic law -- Shariah law. *The Islamic empire will not be limited to just the Spain-to-Indonesia region, for Islamists have a global vision that requires control over non-Muslim countries, also, and specifically the United States.* Their universal ambitions certainly can be stopped, but first they must be understood and resisted. Only when the West, particularly the United States, realizes that the Islamists intend to replace the U.S. Constitution with the Qur'an -- Shariah law -- will it enter the final era of this war -- the Final Jihad.[19]

(emphasis mine)

Referring to the passage of the President's speech in which he points the finger at a *"radical and perverted"* form of Islam that *"rejects tolerance,"* many experts would disagree—citing the fact that the terrorists are, in all reality, practicing Islam as it was meant to be practiced, by adhering to the dictates of the Koran.

Indeed, as illustrated earlier in the chapter addressing the Koran, Allah does not call on Muslims to be accepting of other religions. In fact, to the contrary, he literally requires that Muslims be *intolerant* of other religions: *"So, fight them till all opposition ends and the only religion is Islam"* (Surah 8:39).

Clearly, the terrorists and other fundamentalists are simply following Allah's edict to wage jihad until Islam prevails.

Conclusion

Again, while the average person in the West likely does not have the slightest notion as to what a Caliphate might be, a simple web search will yield innumerable articles, statements, and postings made by Muslim leaders, activists, and citizens—as well as Western commentators.

Remarkably, while disagreement and a general lack of unity have long been hallmarks of the various Islamic factions, the re-establishment of the Caliphate system seems to garner virtually universal support among key Muslim groups and citizens alike.

In an article entitled "Islam's Imperialist Dreams," Efraim Karsh, head of Mediterranean Studies at King's College, is quoted as saying:

> *"Some analysts now see a new "axis of Islam" arising in the Middle East, uniting Hizballah, Hamas, Iran, Syria, the Muslim Brotherhood, elements of Iraq's Shiites, and others in an anti-American, anti-Israel alliance backed by Russia. Whether or not any such structure exists or can be forged, the fact is that the fuel of Islamic imperialism remains as volatile as ever, and is very far from having burned itself out. To deny its force is the height of folly, and to imagine that it can be appeased or deflected is to play into its hands."*[20]

Will a new Islamic Empire become a reality? While some dismiss the notion as an unrealistic pipe dream on the part of Muslim radicals, others see it as a certainty and insist that it is only a matter of time before the world is stunned by the emergence of a revived version of the Caliphate.

Among the Islamic groups that believe the destiny of Islam is to rule the world, there is absolutely no doubt. Like anxious children waiting and planning for Christmas morning, many eager Muslims look forward to the day when *all* citizens will be required to make the oath of allegiance to the Caliph. According to Islamic tradition, those who do not will die the death of an idolater.

PART III

Bible Prophecy and the End Times

While focused primarily on Islam, this book is, in essence, a study of Bible prophecy and how it is being fulfilled. Therefore, it will be helpful to have a basic understanding of how prophecy actually translates into reality. Fortunately, one need only look to recorded history to find numerous examples of this happening.

Thus, in the first of the following two chapters, we will take a look at the past and some of the prophecies that have already been fulfilled; in doing so, we will gain a sense of how things might play out over the years ahead. In the course of our study, it will become apparent that although many of the Bible's predictions are rife with symbolic imagery, the events described are always realized in a very *literal* way.

Secondly, we will explore what the Scriptures have to say about the days directly preceding Christ's return. The "*signs*" detailed in Matthew 24, as well as other passages, seem to indicate that we are living in the days commonly referred to by students of prophecy as the "end times." If we accept this premise—within the context of current world events—it would seem to further the notion that Islam will almost certainly play a prominent role in the days leading up to the end of history as we know it.

SEVEN

"I have declared the former things from the beginning; They went forth from My mouth, and I caused them to hear it. Suddenly I did them, and they came to pass. Even from the beginning I have declared it to you; Before it came to pass I proclaimed it to you, Lest you should say, 'My idol has done them, And my carved image and my molded image Have commanded them.'

—Isaiah 48:3, 5

Bible Prophecy Fulfilled

T
he prophecies of the Old Testament were written centuries
before Christ appeared on the scene. They predicted the location and timing of His birth, the details of His ministry,
and also the nature of His betrayal, death, and burial. All of these
things were spelled out in detail, long before Jesus was born, and
each of them came to pass, exactly as foretold.

The predictions concerning the Messiah's first coming represent but a small percentage of the fulfilled prophecies that both
students and scholars marvel at today.

The fact that these prophecies have inspired so much analysis
and reverence underscores what is, perhaps, the key purpose of fulfilled Bible prophecy: It is through fulfilled prophecy that we can
know that God is "God."

To be sure, among those who have studied the topic, you will
find unanimous agreement that Bible prophecy stands alone in its
ability to accurately predict events that will occur in the future. In
this way, it provides evidence that God exists, and that He is truly
all-knowing and all-powerful.

The fulfillment of Bible prophecy also reminds us that, ultimately, God is in control and that He is bringing His plan to a pre-
announced conclusion in His time and in His way.

It has been said that *"neither man nor demons can hinder
God's plans for the future."* This fact brings comfort to the believer
in an uncertain world.

Facts and Figures

Estimates vary as to the number of prophecies that are contained in the Bible. *The Encyclopedia of Biblical Prophecy* (New

York: Harper & Row, 1973) lists 1,239 prophecies in the Old Testament, and 578 prophecies in the New Testament, for a total of 1,817. These encompass 8,352 verses. Some scholars estimate that one-third of the Scriptures are devoted solely to prophecy—further demonstrating its importance in the eyes of God.

As alluded to in chapter one, in reference to Abraham's descendants, it is interesting to note that the prophecies of the Bible were all delivered by Hebrew prophets. The fact that God chose to reveal His message through one group of people has ensured that we have one reliable source for His Word. Exodus 19:6 further highlights this notion in declaring that the Jews were to be a *"kingdom of priests,"* as they have been chosen to teach the rest of the world about God.

Also noteworthy, is the fact that the prophecies themselves are primarily centered on Israel and refer exclusively to events that take place in the surrounding region. In cases where the prophecies do include other nations, such as Tyre, Babylon, or Edom, it is usually because those nations had sought the destruction of the Jewish people or their homeland, or both.

Is Prophecy Reliable?

Does Bible prophecy offer compelling evidence that vindicates its claim to be the inspired word of God, or is it nothing more than an elaborate hoax? How do the Bible prophecies stand up against recorded history?

The very premise of this book is based on the notion that the Bible's prophecies do, in fact, foretell the future. Indeed, if fulfilled prophecy is simply the result of coincidence, or the overactive imaginations of Bible scholars, then the foundation of the thesis presented here crumbles into nothing.

Fortunately, we have both historical and archaeological evidence that validates the reliability of prophecy. In case after case, recorded history aligns precisely with what the ancient prophecies predicted.

Now, in order to accentuate the remarkable nature of the Bible's prophecies, as well as highlight the shortcomings of counterfeit prophecy, we will begin by taking a look at some of the less trustworthy sources of divination.

False Prophets

All throughout time there have been those who have claimed to have the gift of prophecy. Recently, a well-known debunker of these frauds, James Randi, offered a one million dollar prize to any individual who could, under controlled circumstances, demonstrate any paranormal or supernatural ability. As of yet, no one has passed the preliminary challenge.[1]

Clearly, the record of those who have claimed the gift of "knowing the future" does not hold up very well when compared to the Prophets that God has spoken through. But just in case there was ever any question, God said that we would recognize one of His Prophets, as everything they said about the future would come to pass—one hundred percent of the time. In other words, there was absolutely no allowance made for inaccuracy.

This underscores the notion that the gift of prophecy was taken very seriously in biblical times. In fact, those who were proven to be false prophets were routinely stoned to death.

Success Rates Among Modern Psychics

In the mid-nineties, numerous media outlets reported on a well-documented program that was conducted over a period of more than twenty years.

The CIA and Pentagon spent approximately twenty million dollars to study and employ numerous "psychics." They were supposed to help track down terrorists, find hostages, and assist law enforcement in the war against drugs. Experiments were conducted on such abilities as precognition, clairvoyance, and remote viewing.[2]

The CIA asked two reviewers to evaluate the studies. One was Ray Hyman, a psychology professor at the University of Oregon and a well-known skeptic. The other was Jessica Utts, a statistics professor at the University of California at Davis and an advocate of parapsychology.[3]

Not surprisingly, of the two reviewers, Utts had the more glowing appraisal of the psychic's abilities—testifying that she believed them to be accurate about fifteen percent of the time.[4]

While admittedly, fifteen percent is slightly better than zero percent, we are still unfortunately left with an eighty-five percent failure rate, which, needless to say, would not have met the standard of unqualified accuracy that was required of God's prophets.

What About Nostradamus?

The French physician and astrologer, Nostradamus (1503-1566), penned numerous *quatrains* (four-line stanzas), which were populated by some intriguing yet decidedly ambiguous imagery.

Ever since the publication of Nostradamus' quatrains, his followers have attempted to fit these vague predictions to the events of their times. In some instances, these prophecies might ring somewhat true in that the images employed are so general they can be found in almost any noteworthy event that they are applied to. Yet, the ultimate consequence of this inherent vagueness is that the quatrains never produce a dead-on fit, as the wordings are far too imprecise to be applied to any specific detailed events.[5]

Even so, the general ambiguity of Nostradamus' prophecies has not dissuaded a large number of people from believing in them. It seems that society's need for mysticism runs far too deep to allow this lack of specificity to undermine the credibility of this dubious prophet.

Perhaps driven by this same need, many who search for the certainty of a fulfilled prophecy have been known to get creative by trying to force a fit, often by inventing fanciful translations from the original French—or by asserting that one named term is actually another—in effect, fabricating all or part of the prediction.

In contrast, the Bible's prophecies do not require any manipulation to tie them to the actual historical events that they reference. Thus, we see that Nostradamus' quatrains pale in comparison to the highly specific and accurate nature of the Bible's prophecies.

Why Study Prophecy?

Citing a multitude of reasons, it is virtually unanimous among those who study Bible prophecy that we are living in the end times. In spite of this, many people, having heard the numerous false doomsday predictions, seem to have become somewhat numb to the claim that "the end is near!" and tend to dismiss these beliefs as mere superstition, or something more or less perpetuated by various cult groups or religious fanatics.

Perhaps ironically, this dismissive sentiment, which is commonplace today, was also foretold in the Bible:

> That ye may be mindful of the words which were spoken before by the holy prophets, and of the commandment of us the apostles of the Lord and Savior: Knowing this first, that there shall come in the last days scoffers, walking after their own lusts, And saying, Where is the promise of his coming? for since the fathers fell asleep, all things continue as they were from the beginning of the creation.
>
> —2 Peter 3:2-4

Though written thousands of years ago, this verse demonstrates that God had foreknowledge of the attitudes that would be prevalent in the last days.

As we study this passage, we are reminded that even many of those who believe in the eventuality of Christ's return tend to doubt that this event might actually take place any time soon.

Nonetheless, in answer to those who might question the purpose of studying Bible prophecy, one might argue that if we are actually living in the end times, it would stand to reason that we—more than any generation before us—have a vested interest in learning what the prophecies have to say about the future. The Bible clearly characterizes the last days as a time of great deception, and in order to avoid being among the deceived, one must know what to expect.

"I don't need to know this stuff; I won't be here to see it happen anyway."

Most Churches, today, completely avoid the topic of the end times. This general avoidance of the subject is, in part, due to the fact that many pastors believe the topic will frighten people away; or, in some cases, perhaps church leaders are themselves somewhat uninformed or unsettled on the issue.

Also, not surprisingly, many Christians find the idea of the end times to be somewhat depressing. Human nature being what it is, most of us are not comfortable with radical change, even if it is for the better.

Yet another reason that many have shied away from the topic of the end-times prophecies may be a teaching that gained popularity in the 1830s: The "rapture" is a term that most people are familiar with. It refers to a belief held by many Christians that they will be "*caught up*," or *raptured*, out of the world to be with Jesus, before the time of the great "*tribulation*" begins, which, according to the Bible, will occur during the last several years of history as we know it.

The following verse is often cited as referencing the event that many believe to be the rapture:

> Then we which are alive and remain shall be <u>caught up</u> <u>together with them in the clouds</u>, to meet the Lord in the air: and so shall we ever be with the Lord.
> —1 Thessalonians 4:17

The topic of the rapture is a fairly complex and controversial one and will not be fully examined here. Although, we will note that many scholars, including most of the sources used for this book, disagree with this teaching for numerous reasons; one being, that while there *is* mention of believers being *"caught up,"* it is always done in connection with the return of Christ (at the resurrection). The resurrection will, of course, not take place until the end of the period known as the *"tribulation."*

Providing further evidence that seemingly prohibits a *pre-tribulation* rapture is the following verse, in which the Apostle Paul warns us that the day of Jesus' return will not come until after the man known as the Antichrist is revealed:

> Let no man deceive you by any means: for <u>that day shall not come, except there come a falling away first, and that man of sin be revealed, the son of perdition;</u>
> —2 Thessalonians 2:3

This verse makes it very clear that many will recognize the Antichrist for who he is, most likely as a result of his actions before *"that day"* of Christ's return. Thus, it is safe to assume that believers will not be *raptured*, or taken completely out of harms way as many believe, but will, in fact, be on the earth during the end times—presumably long enough to witness the appearance of the Antichrist and, accordingly, the events of the great tribulation, along with everyone else.

The confusion surrounding this topic stems primarily from the fact that some have interpreted the verse that refers to being *"caught up"* as a unique and separate event that takes place before the resurrection. The aforementioned verse (Thessalonians 4:17) is almost certainly speaking not of a special *rapture* of believers but of the earth-shaking event that the Bible refers to as *"the first resurrection."* It is at this time that *all* of the *living and dead* (in Christ) are raised up. Again, according to the Scriptures, this resurrection will not take place until the *end* of the great tribulation.[6]

It is understandable why many in the church would prefer to avoid the tribulation. The Bible characterizes these days as a time of unprecedented hardship—a brief but brutal period of history like none other. In fact, Mark 13 tells us that things will get so bad that if God were not to intervene and cut these days short, no life would be spared:

> If the Lord had not cut short those days, no one would survive. But for the sake of the elect, whom he has chosen, he has shortened them.
>
> —Mark 13:20

A comforting thought, however, for those who fear being on the earth during those perilous times, is that the resurrection of believers will certainly take place *before* God's Wrath is poured out on the world and the wicked who have rejected Him (Revelation 6:15-17).

Anyone who has studied the Book of Revelation and the events that unfold during this time (of wrath) will tell you that things do get much worse than during the tribulation. Fortunately, this judgment is directed only at those who have rejected God and, for this reason, were not included in the resurrection of believers.

Whatever your beliefs concerning the rapture may be, it is certain that things will become clear at some point. The primary reason for addressing the topic here is that there is a certain danger in assuming that all believers will be removed from the earth before the Antichrist is revealed and the tribulation begins. This expectation serves to lull people into a false sense of security and remove any incentive to learn what the prophecies have to say about the end times.

For instance, many of those who believe in the rapture might consider it a waste of time to study the passages of the Bible that detail the Antichrist's actions against those who reject his authority—believing that they will not be here to witness these atrocities.

Perhaps even more dangerous than the false sense of security that belief in the rapture fosters, is the potential reaction of those who assume that they have been "left behind" to suffer through the tribulation. Indeed, as multitudes of believers awaken to the reality that they have not been "*caught up*" to safety—as they had been taught—there will no doubt be some very distraught and disillusioned Christians.

This may, in fact, turn out to be one of the contributing factors to the great apostasy, or falling away from the faith, that we are warned of in the last days. After all, what could shake one's faith more than believing that they have been deserted by their God, or that the prophecies were wrong? This effect would be further heightened if another religion, perhaps Islam, seemed to be triumphing in the world at a time when so many Christians are suffering great losses.

A Time of Testing?

On the subject of suffering, while many of us cannot imagine that God would let any of His people experience the anguish of the last days, it should be noted that throughout history, God has, at times, allowed His people to face extreme hardship. Sometimes this suffering serves an ultimate purpose that we may not understand but is necessary for our spiritual development. In support of this notion, many Bible scholars believe that one of the primary intents behind the coming tribulation is to refine God's people, much as silver is refined in a furnace. For example, the Book of Daniel speaks of the end times in these terms: "*Many shall be purified, made white, and refined, but the wicked shall do wickedly; and none of the wicked shall understand, but the wise shall understand*" *(Daniel 12:10)*.

To be sure, the tribulation of the end times will serve to separate those who have real faith in God from those who do not. This being the case, it seems likely that all be tested in some respect.

Now, Back to the Topic at Hand

Having addressed the question of whether believers will actually be on the earth to *witness* the fulfillment of the end-times prophecies, we now turn our focus toward the central topic, which is, of course, *fulfilled prophecy*.

Again, our examination of fulfilled prophecy serves a critical purpose: It is by comparing the original prophecy to the actual historical fulfillment that we gain a sense of the language of prophecy and how Scripture translates into literal fulfillment. This being noted, we begin our study by posing a vital question.

Have the Already Fulfilled Prophecies Been Faked?

Many of the more cynical among us may already be wondering if some of the biblical prophecies might have been faked. Is it possible that the scribes who were commissioned to copy the original texts *fudged* the prophecies by adding certain elements or by rewriting them *after* the events actually occurred? The answer to these questions, is simply, no. The ancient hand-written Bible scrolls were copied and distributed far and wide within a very short period of time. It would be virtually impossible for anyone to have collected all of these copies—from Egypt to Babylon—in order to make later modifications.[7]

To illustrate the point, imagine trying to track down all of the copies of a best-selling novel, so that you could make some minor adjustments, *after* it had been published and distributed. It simply could not be done. Invariably, a few copies would slip by, only to turn up at some point in the future, introducing major discrepancies and seriously undermining the credibility of the whole text. This, of course, has not been the case with the Bible.

Further, numerous copies of the Scriptures have been found hidden among ancient artifacts unearthed during archaeological digs, thereby establishing that they were written long before the events that they accurately predicted.

The Dead Sea Scrolls are a prime example of this archaeological evidence. Fragments of every known book of the Old Testament were found inside eleven caves along the northwest shore of the Dead Sea between 1947 and 1956. The scrolls were hidden around the time of the first Jewish revolt in 66-70 A.D., and are dated to have been written in the period from around 200 B.C. to 68 A.D.—well before the time that many of the prophecies contained in them were fulfilled.[8]

For those who require more detailed evidence in support of the authenticity and dating of Bible Scripture, volumes have been written on the subject. For the sake of brevity, we have only touched on the obvious. Nonetheless, we are now prepared to move on to some actual examples of fulfilled prophecy.

Prophecies Fulfilled by Jesus

The Old Testament contains over three hundred passages that refer to the first coming of the Messiah. As alluded to at the beginning of this chapter, Bible scholars have found within these passages, forty-eight specific details about the life, death, and resurrection of Christ. *These prophecies were published five centuries before the historical figure known as Jesus was born in Bethlehem.*

The laws of probability preclude the notion that one man might appear at some point during the course of history and fulfill all of these diverse and highly specific predictions. In fact, many scholars have noted that it would be statistically impossible for one to do so.

We begin, then, with a look at a small sampling of the Old Testament prophecies regarding the coming Messiah, and how they were fulfilled by Jesus.

Prophecy: His hands and feet would be pierced.

For dogs have surrounded Me; The congregation of the

wicked has enclosed Me. <u>They pierced My hands and My feet;</u>

—Psalm 22:16

Fulfillment: As we know, Jesus' hands and feet were pierced through on the cross, but take a moment and consider the following: When this prophecy was first spoken by Israel's King David, crucifixion, as a form of capital punishment, *had not yet been conceived of* by the Persians (from whom this form of torture originated) and it would be yet another thousand years before it was made common by the Romans.[9, 10]

Prophecy: He would be betrayed by Judas for thirty pieces of silver: the price of a slave.

Then I said to them, "If it is agreeable to you, give me my wages; and if not, refrain." So they weighed out for my wages <u>thirty pieces of silver</u>.

—Zechariah 11:12

Fulfillment: What many find so remarkable about this prophecy is that both the price *and* the specific mode of exchange of Jesus' betrayal (thirty pieces of silver) were predicted five hundred years in advance. Assuming that one could predict the price of *anything* five hundred years from now, is it likely that we could also be certain of the form of payment?

Prophecy: His side will be pierced while on the cross.

"And I will pour on the house of David and on the inhabitants of Jerusalem the Spirit of grace and supplication; then they will look on Me <u>whom they pierced</u>. Yes, they will

mourn for Him as one mourns for his only son, and grieve
for Him as one grieves for a firstborn.

—Zechariah 12:10

Fulfillment: Of the three men hanging on the cross that day at
Calvary, Jesus was the only one who had his side pierced by the
Roman soldiers: *"But one of the soldiers pierced His side with a
spear, and immediately blood and water came out" (John 19:34).*

Interestingly, the *"water"* that John witnessed coming from Jesus' side can be explained by two conditions: *pericardial effusion*
and *pleural effusion*, both of which are essentially a collection of
fluid in the membrane around the heart and lungs respectively.[11]
This would be the expected result of a sustained rapid heart rate
brought on by the massive physical trauma that was inflicted upon
Jesus before and during the crucifixion.

Prophecy: None of His bones would be broken

He guards all his bones; Not one of them is broken.

—Psalm 34:20

Fulfillment: During crucifixion, when the Roman soldiers wished
to speed the death of a victim, it was normal practice to break the
prisoner's legs with a club. This prevented the person being crucified from using his legs to lift the body and expand the diaphragm,
allowing air into the lungs.[12] In John 19, we learn that when the
soldiers discovered that Jesus had already died, they did not bother
to break his legs: *"But when they came to Jesus and saw that He
was already dead, they did not break His legs" (John 19:33).*

Prophecy: Darkness would cover the land from the sixth hour until the ninth hour of the day Christ was crucified.

"And it shall come to pass in that day," says the Lord GOD, "That I will make the sun go down at noon, And I will darken the earth in broad daylight;

—Amos 8:9

Fulfillment: This prophecy, in addition to being fulfilled in the pages of the New Testament, is also corroborated by more than one *non-Christian* historian. Notably, the *Third History of Thallus*, penned by an historian of the third century, reported an "*unusual darkness*" that blotted out the sun for several hours at the time of Passover in 32 A.D. (the time of Christ's crucifixion).[13]

The author speculated at the time that the strange darkness was the result of an eclipse. However, astronomers have noted that it was an impossibility for an eclipse to have happened at this time, as Christ died during the season of the paschal full moon. This eliminates any chance that the darkness was a naturally occurring coincidence.

Yet another non-Christian historian, Phlegon, wrote a history called *Chronicles*, which also parallels the biblical account—further demonstrating that this bizarre occurrence, in which darkness fell upon the land, was widely acknowledged throughout the non-Christian world, thus requiring a naturalistic explanation from these secular historians.[14]

Having noted only a few of the prophecies that were fulfilled by Jesus, we now turn to some of the Old Testament prophecies which were spoken in regard to the Nation of Israel.

Prophecies Fulfilled in Regard to Israel

Prophecy: The Jews would have a worldwide impact.

And I will make of thee a great nation, and I will bless thee, and make thy name great; and thou shalt be a blessing: And I will bless them that bless thee, and curse him

86

that curseth thee: and in thee shall all families of the earth
be blessed.

—Genesis 12:2-3

Fulfillment: Aside from their well-documented history of persecution, the Jewish people are truly blessed in many ways. They are unrivaled in the impact that they have had on the world. As a matter of fact, if you were to write down a list of the most influential people in theology, governance, philosophy, music, science, literature, and commerce, it would become very apparent that the Jewish people figure prominently, in spite of the fact that they are disproportionately small in number—representing less than one percent of the earth's population.

Further, we note that the middle part of this verse speaks to the notion that those who bless Israel will be rewarded, while those who curse her will be punished. It is, perhaps, very telling to assess the current status of the nations that have historically "cursed" Israel, as compared to the primarily Western nations (in particular the U.S.) that have been a friend to this tiny country. Indeed, the overall well-being of a nation and its citizens does actually appear to be associated to the nature of its relationship with Israel.

Prophecy: Old Jerusalem and the Temple would be destroyed.

The heads thereof judge for reward, and the priests thereof teach for hire and the prophets thereof divine for money: yet will they lean upon the LORD, and say, Is not the LORD among us? none evil can come upon us. There-fore shall Zion for your sake be plowed as a field, and Je-rusalem shall become heaps, and the mountain of the house as the high places of the forest.

—Micah 3:11-12

Fulfillment: Twenty-seven centuries ago, the Prophet Micah said that Jerusalem would be destroyed and that Zion (a central part of Jerusalem) would be "*plowed as a field.*"

Since the time of Micah, the city of Jerusalem has been destroyed three times: once by the Babylonians in 586 B.C.—followed by the Romans, who destroyed the city twice—once in 70 A.D., and again in 135 A.D.

According to a text in the *Gemara* (an ancient Jewish writing), the Romans *literally ran a plow over Zion* on the ninth day of the Jewish month, Ab. The Gemara further specifies that Turnus Rufus (a Roman officer) was responsible for the plowing of the Temple.

Additionally, there was a Roman coin minted during the era of Hadrian (the Roman general who destroyed Jerusalem in 135 A.D.) that shows an image of a man riding a plow over Jerusalem. This coin is said to have been minted to commemorate the founding of the pagan Roman city called "Aelia Capitolina" on top of the ruins of Jerusalem.[15]

Prophecy: The Jews would be scattered world wide.

And the LORD shall scatter thee among all people, from the one end of the earth even unto the other; and there thou shalt serve other gods, which neither thou nor thy fathers have known, even wood and stone. And among these nations shalt thou find no ease, neither shall the sole of thy foot have rest: but the LORD shall give thee there a trembling heart, and failing of eyes, and sorrow of mind:
—Deuteronomy 28:64, 65

Fulfillment: Many Jews were forced out of their homeland by the conquering Assyrians approximately 2,700 years ago and then, again, by the Babylonians a century or so later; yet, many managed to return.

Finally, the Roman destruction of Jerusalem and the Temple in the first century A.D. would wipe out the very center of Jewish worship, leading to a worldwide dispersion of the Jews.[16]

Prophecy: The Jews would return to, and thrive in, their ancient homeland.

> That then the LORD thy God will turn thy captivity, and have compassion upon thee, and will return and gather thee from all the nations, whither the LORD thy God hath scattered thee. If any of thine be driven out unto the outmost parts of heaven, from thence *will the LORD thy* God gather thee, and from thence will he fetch thee: And the LORD thy God will bring thee into the land which thy fathers possessed, and thou shalt possess it; and he will do thee good, and multiply thee above thy fathers.
>
> —Deuteronomy 30:3-5

Fulfillment: During the late 1800s, after nearly seventeen centuries of exile, the Jews began to return to their ancient homeland. At the time, the land was called Palestine and was ruled over by the Ottoman Empire.

Shortly before and also after the Holocaust of World War Two, a few million more returned to the land of their forefathers.

When the Jews finally re-claimed ownership of Israel in 1948, it was the first time in nearly 2,000 years that they had claimed sovereignty over any part of their homeland. It was also the first time in 2,900 years that Israel was both a united and sovereign country. No nation has ever endured such a lengthy interval separated from its homeland—let alone while facing the additional challenge of having its residents exiled and scattered throughout the world.

Prophecy: The Nation of Israel would be born in *one day*.

> Who hath heard such a thing? who hath seen such things?
> Shall the earth be made to bring forth in one day? <u>or shall
> a nation be born at once</u>? for as soon as Zion travailed,
> she brought forth her children.
>
> —Isaiah 66:8

Fulfillment: In Isaiah 66:8, the Prophet speaks of a country being born in one day. This accurately describes what happened on May 14, 1948, when the Jews declared independence for Israel. During that same day, the United States issued a statement recognizing Israel's sovereignty; while, only hours beforehand, a United Nations mandate expired, ending British control of the land. Therefore, during a twenty-four hour span of time, foreign control of the Land of Israel had formally ceased, Israel had declared its independence, and its independence was acknowledged by other nations. True to God's promise, modern Israel was literally born in a single day.[17]

Prophecy: Israel would experience her birth pains *after* she was born.

> <u>Before she travailed</u>, she brought forth; <u>before her pain
> came</u>, she was delivered of a man child.
>
> —Isaiah 66:7

Fulfillment: In what might be characterized as a reversal of the natural order of things, Isaiah said that the birth of Israel would take place *before* there would be labor pains. Again, history confirms that this is precisely what happened.

When the Jews declared sovereignty over Israel in 1948, the declaration did not follow a war for independence, as is common when a new nation is born. In this case, a war for independence came immediately *after* the declaration of sovereignty. Oddly enough, the birth was peaceful, and the aftermath was painful: Within hours of the establishment of Israel as a nation, she was attacked by Egypt, Jordan, Syria, Lebanon, Iraq, and Saudi Arabia.[18] Israel, against all odds, not only prevailed in this war but expanded the size of the country by fifty percent.

Prophecy: God would restore Hebrew as the spoken language in Israel.

> "For then I will return to the people a <u>pure language</u>, that they may all call upon the name of the Lord, to serve him with one consent."
>
> —Zephaniah 3:9

Fulfillment: Prior to the restoration of Israel in 1948, Hebrew was a dead language. In 1982, Hebrew became the official language of Israel and is now spoken throughout the nation.

The History of the Jews: Proof of God?

The prophecies concerning Israel serve to underscore the miraculous story of the Jewish people. It is perhaps not surprising, then, that when asked for proof of the existence of God, many Bible scholars will simply answer, "The Jews."

Given the history of this relatively small group of people, this answer does not seem unreasonable. Throughout the centuries, the Jews have been a constant target of persecution. Driven from their homeland and scattered over the face of the globe, they have not only maintained their identity as a people but have somehow managed to make their way back to the land of their forefathers to regain status as a nation.

Today, the Jewish people have turned what had become a desolate wasteland into a blossoming oasis in the desert. In the face of overwhelming odds, they have prevailed in several wars against the Arab nations that surround them. And finally, in spite of the obstacles that they have faced, the Jews have contributed enormously to the well being of humanity in all arenas.

Thus, the Jews stand as a testament to the truth of Bible prophecy, as the recorded history of this people parallels, to the letter, what God had ordained thousands of years ago in the Scriptures.

Prophecies Concerning Other Nations

In addition to the Messianic prophecies and those concerning Israel, the Bible is filled with predictions concerning the nations that surround this tiny piece of land.

Some of the most amazingly accurate and detailed prophecies come from the Book of Daniel. For instance, in Daniel 11:1-9 we find a concise history of the Near East: From Alexander the Great, to Antiochus the Great, the key events of this time period were spelled out hundreds of years prior to the time that they actually took place.

Unable to explain away the incredible accuracy of Daniel's predictions, skeptics often resort to discrediting the book itself by claiming that the entire thing was a "fraud," written only *after* the prophecies it details were fulfilled. Yet, as we will see, Daniel has been verified by outside sources to have been written long before the events that it describes.

Let us look, then, to one example of Daniel's prophecies concerning a world renowned conqueror, whose life is thoroughly documented in the annals of secular history.

Daniel Predicts the Fall of Alexander the Great and the Dividing of the Greek Empire

One of Daniel's most extraordinary prophecies was his description of the fall of Alexander the Great and the dividing of the Greek Empire. The proof that these prophecies were recorded long before their fulfillment comes from the Jewish historian, Flavius Josephus (court historian for three successive Roman emperors).

Josephus tells us that Alexander the Great actually *received a copy* of the Book of Daniel upon his annexation of Jerusalem in the autumn of 332 B.C. (Antiquities of the Jews XI, chapter viii, paragraphs 3-5). Therefore, the writings of Josephus provide reliable outside testimony that dates the Book of Daniel to *before* 332 B.C. The extraordinary thing, however, is that unbeknownst to Alexander, his own fate was chronicled within the pages of Daniel 8, including the future division of the Grecian Empire among his four generals following his death, as well as the coming of the Roman Empire, which would take place years after Alexander's day.

History tells us that Alexander grew to be one of the most powerful men on earth; some would say the greatest military leader the world has ever known. Even so, he died in 323 B.C., without having organized and consolidated the nations that he had conquered into a cohesive empire. Consequently, Alexander's generals began to vie for power amongst themselves.

In less than fifteen months, his half-brother and his two sons had been murdered—leaving the Empire without a leader. None of Alexander's men had the authority or leadership prowess required to replace him by themselves, so his four generals split up the Empire: In the East, Seleucus obtained Syria, Babylonia, and Media; in the West, Cassander, took Macedon Thessaly, and Greece; in the South, Ptolemy, procured Egypt, and Cyprus; and in the North, Lysimachus secured Thrace and Cappadocia, in addition to the north parts of Asia Minor. Amazingly, this complex web of historical events unfolded precisely as was foretold in the Book of Daniel.

As we conclude our study of fulfilled Bible prophecy, we look to one last example that showcases the characteristic accuracy and detail of these ancient predictions.

Ezekiel Foretells the Fate of a Great City

In the Book of Ezekiel, chapter 26:1-12, we find an astonishingly clear description of the fate of a city called Tyre. Again, not surprisingly, the Bible's account correlates precisely with what the historical record tells us about the destiny of this city.

Tyre was no small, obscure village. It was a great Phoenician city and a world capital for over two thousand years. Still, in the heyday of its power, the Prophet Ezekiel had the audacity to predict this city's violent future and ultimate destruction. This downfall would be due to the flagrant wickedness and arrogance of Tyre—traits that were personified in its ruler, Ittobal II, who claimed to be God.

Ezekiel prophesied that many nations would come up against Tyre, and that specifically Babylon (under Nebuchadnezzar) would be the first to attack it. He also predicted that Tyre's walls and towers would be broken down and that the stones, timbers, and debris of the great city would be thrown into the sea. The Prophet further described the degree to which the city would be humbled by predicting that its location would become nothing more than a bare rock and a place for the drying of fishermen's nets. Lastly, Ezekiel informs us that the city of Tyre would *never again* be rebuilt.

History bears testimony to the fact that all of this is precisely what happened. Many nations did come up against Tyre: the Babylonians, the Greeks, the Romans, and also the Muslims, to name a few. As was foretold in the Scriptures, Babylon's Nebuchadnezzar was the first of these invaders. True to the prophecy, after a thirteen year siege, the Babylonians broke down the walls and towers of mainland Tyre, in this way, fulfilling the first part of Ezekiel's prediction. Nebuchadnezzar massacred all of Tyre's inhabitants, except for those who had escaped to an island fortress located a half mile out in the Mediterranean Sea.

Centuries after Ezekiel's predictions had been recorded, Alexander the Great fulfilled another major portion of the prophecy: In order to conquer the island fortress of Tyre—without the luxury of a navy—he and his celebrated architect, Diades, devised one of the most brilliant engineering feats of ancient warfare. They built a causeway from Tyre's mainland to the island fortress using the millions of cubic feet of rubble left over on mainland Tyre. In the process, Tyre was scraped as bare as a rock, just as Ezekiel had predicted.

Perhaps the most astonishing of Ezekiel's predictions was that Tyre would never be rebuilt. This is particularly remarkable, as it sits on a prime piece of real estate: Located on the east coast of the Mediterranean Sea, Tyre contains the Springs of Reselain, which pump ten million gallons of fresh water daily—enough to take care of the needs of a modern city. Yet, history records that after a succession of invasions, Tyre finally and irrevocably fell in A.D. 1,291—never to be rebuilt again.

Today, Tyre has been humbled to the point of becoming a place for the drying of fishermen's nets, just as Ezekiel prophesied 2,500 years ago.

Again, the prophecy regarding Tyre, as well as the others that we have examined here, are but a few among scores of fulfilled Bible prophecies—any one of which is sufficient to demonstrate the truth and accuracy of the Scriptures.

As God assures us in John 10, no prophecy will go unfulfilled: *"I have spoken," says the Lord of Hosts. The Scripture cannot be broken (John 10:35).*

EIGHT

The Pharisees also with the Sadducees came, and testing, desired Him that He would show them a sign from Heaven. He answered and said unto them, "When it is evening ye say, 'It will be fair weather, for the sky is red.' And in the morning, 'It will be foul weather today, for the sky is red and lowering.' O ye hypocrites, ye can discern the face of the sky, but can ye not discern the signs of the times?

—Matthew 16:1-3

Signs of the Times

S poken of in scores of passages throughout the Scriptures, taught in parables and explained in the most vivid and varied of ways, the return of Jesus Christ to this earth promises to be the most breathtaking and glorious event ever to be witnessed by mankind.

Indeed, the awesome significance of the Second Coming completely dwarfs all other worldly concerns. Yet, strangely enough, the vast majority of the population appears to be utterly oblivious to the fact that this world-changing event looms just over the horizon.

Most people correctly sense that the international situation seems to be worsening by the moment—and with no clear resolution in sight—but *why* this is all happening and *how* it will ultimately be resolved remains a complete mystery to them.

And so, for the masses, the never-ending stream of troublesome news that flows forth from the media each day serves only to instill a chronic sense of apprehension.

An Unheeded Warning

It is often said that *"to be forewarned is to be forearmed."* In other words, knowledge of imminent danger can enable us to sufficiently prepare for it. To illustrate, if a neighbor was tracking recent storm movements and had foreknowledge of an approaching tornado, most of us would want that neighbor to share this information—and the sooner the better—so that we might have the opportunity to make preparations.

The circumstances in our world today are much the same, albeit it on a much larger scale. Some have seen the signs and know what is coming but too many have not and are, therefore, hopelessly unprepared.

Living in an Age of Skepticism

In addition to those who are simply unaware, there are also many *believers* who express doubts as to whether we are truly approaching the end of the age. As noted in the previous chapter, some dismiss the whole notion as simply a "fairy tale" that has been cooked up by "fanatics," who have, for some odd reason, determined that the Bible is to be interpreted "literally."

To be honest, considering that man has been predicting the end of the world for almost as long as the Scriptures have been in existence, some of this cynicism is understandable—as, contrary to the numerous claims that "the end is near," the world keeps spinning, and life as we know it continues, just as it has from the beginning.

Nevertheless, for those who believe that the Bible predicts the future, and that its message should be taken at face value, it is not a question of if the day will come but merely of *when*. And while the question of timing does remain, God has by no means left us in the dark concerning this matter.

What Does the Bible Say?

Some might be surprised to learn that in the Bible Jesus actually gives us a complete list of some very specific signs that we are to look for—signs that signal the time of His coming as being very near.

The passages known as the *Olivet Discourse*, contained in both Matthew 24 and Mark 13, offer the most straightforward teaching in regard to the end times found anywhere in the Bible and are, in fact, the very cornerstone of New Testament eschatology. Found within these verses are the definitive signs that Jesus tells His followers to watch for, just prior to His second coming at the end of the age.

Signs Given by Jesus to Indicate That the Time of His Return Is Near

In Matthew 24:3 Jesus is asked, *"Tell us, when will these things be, and what will be the sign of your coming, and of the end of the age?"* In addressing the *"end of the age,"* Jesus compares these days to a woman who is in labor; the obvious parallel being that when a woman's labor pains begin, she knows that the child will soon be born.

False prophets, wars, famine, pestilence, and earthquakes are all described as birth pains which herald the beginning of the end of history as we know it. Many Bible scholars agree that most, if not all, of these signs, have, to some extent, already been fulfilled. In other words, one might say that the "minimum requirements" have been met. Even so, as we get closer to the end, all of these signs will become even more pronounced, and increasingly obvious, to those who recognize them for what they are.

With these things in mind, let us take a closer look at the specific signs that we are given in the Bible, and examine the ways in which each of them are being manifested in today's world.

We begin with Christ's prophetic warning of forthcoming imposters and frauds.

False Prophets and Christs

For many shall come in my name, saying, I am Christ; and shall deceive many.

—Matthew 24:5

A February 2007 article posted on CNN.com profiled a man named Jose Luis de Jesus Miranda, who claims to be God. Jose teaches his followers that there is no devil and no sin. His church claims thousands of followers from more than thirty countries.[1]

Today, bizarre stories like this one are not rare. In the 1990s, a Syracuse University professor, who researched the contemporary religious landscape in America, estimated that there were well over two thousand practicing gurus calling themselves Christ.[2]

False "prophets" are also plentiful in our day. Some examples may include certain church leaders or charismatic televangelists who, on the surface, proclaim to deliver Christ's message but, in truth, deliver their own false doctrine.

As the end of the age approaches and we enter into the period known as the "*tribulation*," Jesus warns that these false prophets and messiahs will become even more numerous and deceptive—misleading multitudes: "*At that time if anyone says to you, 'Look, here is the Christ!' or, 'There he is!' do not believe it.*" *(Matthew 24:26)*

In verse 27, Jesus goes on to detail the nature of His appearance so that His followers will not be deceived: "*For as lightning that comes from the east is visible even in the west, so will be the coming of the Son of Man.*"

Wars and Rumors of Wars

And ye shall hear of <u>wars and rumors of wars</u>: see that ye be not troubled: for all these things must come to pass, but the end is not yet.

—Matthew 24:6

No generation in all of history has ever witnessed the dramatic escalation of warfare that we have seen over the last hundred years. The International Red Cross estimates that over one hundred million people have been killed in wars since the twentieth century began.[3]

As the instability in the Middle East and other areas around the world escalates, more and more nations work feverishly to develop nuclear weapons. Add to that the unpredictable nature of many of today's world leaders, and the potential for yet more conflicts is vastly compounded.

As for "*rumors*" of potential wars, they have become commonplace in recent years and now appear in the headlines daily—

perhaps most notably, the ongoing rumors of an imminent confrontation with Iran. Another example would be, of course, the long-standing Arab threat to "wipe Israel off of the map."

Significantly, it is only in relatively recent history that mankind has developed the technology to allow instantaneous access to these *"rumors,"* or forecasts of war, which loom ever presently on the horizon.

Famines, Pestilence and Earthquakes

> For nation shall rise against nation, and kingdom against kingdom: and there shall be <u>famines, and pestilences, and earthquakes, in divers places</u>.
>
> —Matthew 24:7

This verse mentions three major types of calamity, each of which qualifies as a major event on its own. Thus, we will address each of them individually.

Famines:

It is estimated by the World Health Organization that one-third of the world is well-fed, one-third is under-fed, and one-third is starving.[4] In spite of advanced irrigation and farming technology, according to a 2004 report released by the U.N. Food and Agricultural Agency (FAO), the number of people who do not get enough to eat has increased to 852 million. This is up eighteen million from the 1990s.[5]

Moreover, in early spring of 2008, the media began reporting on what experts are calling a "global food shortage." Soaring demand, rising oil prices and government mandated biofuel development (intended to reduce oil dependence) have sent commodity prices to their highest levels in history. The impact is being felt most in the developing world, as food riots have erupted in Niger, Senegal, Cameroon, and Burkina Faso, as well as Haiti. Also, protests have flared in Morocco, Mauritania, Ivory Coast, Egypt, Mexico, and Yemen.[6]

The United Nations predicts that increasing food prices will make it even more difficult to meet international goals of reducing hunger. The higher costs are squeezing food-aid budgets that were already falling far behind, due to the increase in war and weather related disasters. The head of the International Monetary Fund, Dominique Strauss-Kahn, warns of widespread starvation and economic disruption if food prices continue to rise.[7]

Pestilence:

A pestilence is defined as any virulent and highly infectious disease that can cause an epidemic or even a pandemic. Ominously, at least thirty *previously unknown* diseases have appeared globally since 1973, including HIV-AIDS, Hepatitis-C, Ebola, hemorrhagic fever, and others. Further, twenty well-known infectious diseases, such as tuberculosis, malaria, and cholera, have re-emerged or spread since 1973—some appearing in deadlier, *drug-resistant* forms.

It should be noted that less than twenty years ago the medical profession claimed victory over a wide array of bacterial and viral killers; but instead of fading, the cases of infectious diseases have skyrocketed throughout the 1990s. Doctors now warn that the current resurgence of drug-resistant bacteria strains could prove to be more deadly than AIDS. Additionally, drug-resistant strains of microbes are having a deadly impact on the fight against tuberculosis, malaria, diarrhea, and pneumonia, which together kill more than ten million people each year.

AIDS is the fourth leading global cause of death. According to UNAIDS, at the end of 1999, over thirty-four million adults and children worldwide were living with HIV-AIDS. In spite of massive efforts directed toward prevention, more than five million people are newly infected each year. Tragically, there are now sixteen countries in which more than one-tenth of the adult population aged fifteen to forty-nine is infected with HIV.[8]

Earthquakes:

The topic of earthquakes, as it turns out, is a broad one; and in light of some recent headlines, it merits some additional focus.

Many scholars believe that Matthew 24 is speaking primarily of *notable* earthquakes that will occur in *"diverse,"* or *various*, locations—thereby assuming that the verse is not necessarily referring to an increase in the volume of earthquake events but rather to varied and widespread occurrences.

Nevertheless, according to some sources, the volume and intensity of earthquakes this century is at a higher level than at any other time in history. Although some would argue that the rise in volume correlates with the increased number of monitoring stations, data from the U.S. Geological Survey National Earthquake Information Center shows that notable earthquakes (6.0 and higher) have increased in number every year, from the years 1970 through 2003.[9]

Yet, there is more to this story. If we take a closer look at the word translated as *"earthquakes"* in Matthew 24, we learn that the Greek word used in the original Bible manuscripts was *seismos*, from which we derive such English words as *seismic* and *seismology*. These terms commonly refer to earthquake activity and the study of earthquakes. Though, interestingly enough, Strong's Lexicon defines *seismos* as *"a commotion, i.e. (of the air) a gale, (of the ground) an earthquake—earthquake, tempest."* This definition clearly implies that the Greek word *seismos* encompasses a much broader meaning than just the earth shaking.[10]

We see more evidence of this in Matthew 8, which records the well-known story of how a violent storm overtook Jesus and His disciples on the Sea of Galilee—threatening to capsize their fishing boat and drown them—until Jesus miraculously calmed the wind and waves. The Greek word used in verse 23 for this sudden, powerful storm is, again, *seismos*—which, in this particular case, is translated to English as a *"great tempest."*[11]

Further still, the parallel account (recorded in Mark 4:37) of the same incident on the Sea of Galilee calls it a *"great storm of wind."* These two references confirm that the word *seismos* also denotes *violent storms involving wind and water.* We can therefore conclude—based on the original Greek text—that the Scriptures, in addition to predicting earthquakes, also foretell hurricanes, typhoons and cyclones, as well as tsunamis, which are, of course, earthquake driven waves.[12]

In light of this additional insight into Matthew 24, we note some compelling statistics that can be found in the September 2005 issue of *Science* magazine. Significantly, research from the Georgia Institute of Technology, and the National Center for Atmospheric Research in Boulder, Colorado, found that the frequency of the most dangerous and damaging storms—those rated category four and five—has *increased by eighty percent* from the 1970s to the last decade.

In another recent study (compiled from Red Cross data and conducted by the U.N., along with specialist researchers at Louvain University in Belgium), findings show that floods and windstorms have increased from sixty events in 1980, to two hundred and forty events in 2004, with flooding itself up six-fold. Additionally, the study found that the number of people affected by extreme natural disasters has surged by almost seventy percent: from 174 million a year, between 1985 and 1994, to 254 million people a year, between 1995 and 2004.[13]

These statistics point to a tremendous increase in storm activity. In fact, we have in recent years experienced some of the most devastating natural disasters in recorded history. To further underscore the extent of this increase, we take note of two recent and very well-known examples of storm events.

— The Sumatra Tsunami:

The greatest tsunami in recent history occurred off the coast of

Sumatra in 2004. This massive series of waves was caused by an underwater earthquake that was recorded to have a magnitude of 9.2 on the Richter scale. The official death toll is not known but is estimated at somewhere between 200,000 and 300,000 people. The devastation that was left, and the clean up that followed, is unprecedented when compared to any natural disaster event in modern times.[14]

— Hurricane Katrina:

The hurricane season of 2005 was the most active Atlantic hurricane season ever recorded—repeatedly shattering previous records. The impact of the 2005 season was widespread and devastating, with at least 2,280 deaths and record damages of over 128 billion dollars.[15]

The most deadly of the storms, Hurricane Katrina, caused catastrophic damage to the Gulf Coast—unleashing a thirty foot storm surge that devastated a long stretch of coastline along Louisiana, Mississippi, and Alabama. Katrina was the costliest hurricane in U.S. history—surpassing 1992s Hurricane Andrew—and also the deadliest hurricane in the U.S. since 1928.[16]

— Predictions of Increasing Storms:

In March of 2007, leading meteorologists, who attended a conference hosted by the World Meteorological Organization, ominously predicted a continuing increase in tidal waves, floods, and hurricanes. Speaking at the four day conference, the Secretary General of the organization, Michel Jarraud, had this to say:

"What we know is that global warming is very likely to lead in the future to more frequent tidal waves...Heavy precipitation events are very likely to become more frequent...and it's likely that hurricanes and cyclones will become more intense..."[17]

While many attribute the staggering increase of these natural disasters to global warming—which may or may not be the case—these calamities, from a biblical perspective, are simply the fulfillment of what was foretold nearly two thousand years ago: "...*On the earth, nations will be in anguish and perplexity at the roaring and tossing of the sea*" *(Luke 21:25)*.

As highlighted earlier, these first five signs should be recognized as the birth pains, or the "*the beginning of sorrows*" *(Matthew 24:8)*. These events will all increase in intensity and severity as the time of the end approaches.

This being noted, we return to Matthew 24, for yet more signs of Christ's return.

Tribulations

Then shall they deliver you up to be afflicted, and shall kill you: and ye shall be hated of all nations for my name's sake.

—Matthew 24:9

Though we do not hear much about it from the mainstream media, Christians are under attack throughout the world today. One such example being the current state of affairs in Indonesia, where Muslims are attempting to establish the foundation of a southeast Caliphate from which to launch attacks against neighboring nations.[18]

Consequently, *tens of thousands* of Christians have reportedly been killed by Muslims. Notable among these murders, is a 2005 incident in which several teenage girls were attacked and beheaded while en route to a Christian school that they attended.[19]

There are also innumerable accounts of Churches and Christian villages being burned to the ground by Muslim mobs.

Similar atrocities are playing out in many other Muslim (and non-Muslim) nations around the globe. One need only consult the *New Foxe's Book of Martyrs* for further examples of the death and affliction that Christians are suffering for their faith.

As the time of the end approaches, this persecution will increase, and many more will be martyred for their beliefs.

The Gospel Will be Preached Throughout the Whole World

> And this gospel of the kingdom shall be preached in all the world for a witness unto all nations; and then shall the end come.
>
> —Matthew 24:14

Obviously, there is no practical way for one to determine at which point the gospel has been preached to every nation and to God's complete satisfaction. However, there is now, and has been for quite some time, a massive effort toward "the great completion." With the benefit of today's communications technology, including internet, radio, and television—all things that did not exist until the twentieth century—the process of spreading the gospel to *all* nations has been vastly accelerated in this generation.

"...So we're close, but how close?"

While the combination of these signs serve to alert us that we are nearing the time of Christ's return, some may reason that one cannot conclude with absolute certainty at which point a particular sign should be considered *fulfilled*—in this manner, calling into question the notion that one might determine with utter certainty that we are living in the last days.

Perhaps seeking to sustain this air of uncertainty, many refer to Jesus' own words from Matthew 24 in support of the idea that no one will know the time of His coming:

> But of <u>that day and hour </u>knoweth no man, no, not the angels of heaven, but my Father only.
>
> —Matthew 24:36

Indeed, in verse 36, Jesus specifically tells His disciples that *"no man"* will know the *"day and hour"* of His return. Yet, it is interesting to note that He purposefully limits His statement to *"that day and hour."* Citing this fact, many interpret the verse in a literal sense, taking it to mean only that we cannot know the *exact "day and hour"* of His return. In light of this, many have reasoned that the possibility of determining the general timeframe, season, or perhaps, even the month or week of Jesus' coming is not precluded by this statement.

While this may seem like splitting hairs to some, it has been demonstrated through studying fulfilled prophecy that God has chosen His words carefully when revealing the future—and when analyzing such verses, details like this should not be overlooked.

Therefore, although this verse from Matthew 24 leaves us with the impression that we may not know the precise timing of Christ's return, it is quite likely—perhaps even certain—that many who are watching will recognize when the time is at hand.

Nevertheless, for those who are looking for something a little more concrete, many Bible scholars believe that in addition to the aforementioned signs, we are given a very clear milestone to watch for—in this case, something with a specific date attached to it.

The Parable of the Fig Tree

In Mark 13, we find the passage known as the *"parable of the fig tree."* Many scholars believe that in these verses Jesus gets much more specific and alludes to a very definite time frame in which He will return. In fact, it is believed that He references a distinct event that we might pinpoint on the calendar and then associate with a specific length of time—that length of time being one generation:

Now learn a parable of the fig tree; <u>When her branch is yet tender, and putteth forth leaves, ye know that summer is near:</u> So ye in like manner, <u>when ye shall see these</u>

110

things come to pass, know that it is nigh, even at the doors. Verily I say unto you, that this generation shall not pass, till all these things be done.

—Mark 13:28-30

To fully appreciate what Jesus was telling His disciples, we must first understand what, if anything, was implied in His reference to the budding of the fig tree. In other words, was it simply used in a metaphorical sense to suggest a way in which we might recognize a general change in *season*, or was it intended to represent something more specific?

In answer to this, many scholars have concluded that the referenced *"fig tree"* is almost certainly representative of the Nation of Israel and that the tender branch which *"putteth forth new leaves"* symbolizes its rebirth as a state on May 14, 1948.

Numerous Bible verses have been cited in support of this theory. For instance, in Matthew 21:18-22, we note that as Jesus was entering the city, He saw a fig tree that had lots of leaves but no fruit; He cursed it, saying, *"Let no fruit grow on thee hence forward forever,"* and the tree withered away. Many scholars have proposed that since the fig tree was showing leaves, it gave the appearance of being fruitful from a distance, but upon closer examination it became clear that there was no real fruit at all. These same scholars suggest that perhaps Jesus' cursing of the fig tree was an acted out parable in which He used the fig tree to represent Israel—thereby teaching the disciples that God will judge those who give an outer appearance of fruitfulness but, in fact, are not spiritually fruitful. This was most definitely the case with many of the Jews in Israel at the time.

Some scholars also cite the non-canonical (not included in the Bible) Apocalypse of Peter, in which Peter discusses the significance of the fig tree with Jesus, who states that the fig tree represents "the House of Israel."

Further support for Israel as the fig tree is found in the Old Testament; examples include Jeremiah 24, Joel chapter 1, Hosea chapter 9 and Micah 4, among a host of others.

Now, then, having built a solid case that the fig tree is frequently used to represent Israel in the Scriptures, we return to Mark 13, where Jesus reveals some crucial information. He tells His disciples that *"this generation,"* meaning the generation that witnesses the *specific signs* given earlier—along with the *budding of the fig tree*—would not pass away *"till all these things be done,"* or until all of the prophecies that pertain to the end are fulfilled. In other words, the generation that is alive to see the rebirth of Israel and the specific signs given in Matthew 24 will also be alive on the earth at the time of Christ's return.

Assuming that the interpretation is correct, the only missing piece of the puzzle would appear to be the actual length of time denoted by a *biblical* generation. If we were to suppose that a generation—based on the average life span—is approximately eighty years, then one could simply begin at 1948 and add eighty in order to establish a definite window of time. However, when interpreting Scripture, one should not assume anything. The question, then, is how might we determine the number of years Jesus was alluding to when He spoke of a *"generation?"*

Unfortunately, Bible scholars differ in their opinions as to the length of time implied by the term *generation*. The theories vary from forty to seventy and even up to one hundred and twenty years. Based on the Scriptures, a case could be made for each of these figures.

Considering this, it seems unlikely that anyone will arrive at the exact number of years implied with absolute certainty. Nonetheless, the point to be made is that even though we may not, at present, be able to determine a *precise* span of time, we have the common understanding that a generation is a relatively small number of years—as any senior citizen will tell you.

Thus, in light of the rebirth of Israel and the insight provided by both Mark 13 and Matthew 24, even a cursory glimpse of the world today would seem to support the notion that we are, in fact, living in the times that Jesus spoke of. This being the case, there is no reason that one should not be able to recognize the signs of the times and determine that *"summer is near."*

As we conclude our study of the *Olivet Discourse*, we look to the Books of Timothy, Daniel, and Luke, for some other key characteristics of the last days.

Other General Characteristics of the Last Days

But know this, that in the last days perilous times will come: For men will be lovers of themselves, lovers of money, boasters, proud, blasphemers, disobedient to parents, unthankful, unholy, unloving, unforgiving, slanderers, without self-control, brutal, despisers of good, traitors, headstrong, haughty, lovers of pleasure rather than lovers of God, having a form of godliness but denying its power. And from such people turn away!

—2 Timothy 3:1-5, 7

For anyone who has watched television, read a newspaper, lost a retirement to corporate greed and corruption—or just walked out of their front door lately—it is obvious that this prophecy has been fulfilled in the current generation.

For those who are at least forty years old, I ask that you take a moment and consider each of the traits that are listed in this verse. Next, form a mental image of the various aspects of society—including entertainment, cultural, and family—as they existed just three decades ago; then do the same for our present day society. In comparing these two images, it becomes clear that we are not living in the same world that existed just thirty years ago. Predictably, the further back in recent history one looks, the more obvious the contrast becomes.

While people such as these have always been with us, it is beyond evident that these attributes have become much more prevalent in our time. Many experts cite the breakdown of the basic family structure as a root cause.

Apostasy (Falling Away From the Faith)

For the time will come when men will not put up with sound doctrine. Instead, to suit their own desires, <u>they will gather around them a great number of teachers to say what their itching ears want to hear.</u>

—2 Timothy 4:3

Due, in part, to today's "all-inclusive" environment, many churches are straying ever further from preaching the Word of God as it is written in the Bible and are, instead, embracing *new age* or *interfaith* agendas, which, in many cases, deny Christ as the only way to salvation.

In a 2005 interview with Larry King, one of the most well-known pastors of our day, Joel Osteen, repeatedly dodged King's question about whether Jews, Muslims, Atheists, or those who do not accept Christ at all, will go to heaven. Osteen repeatedly answered with, "I don't know," saying it is not his business and that he is very careful about judging who would, and who would not, go to heaven.[20]

While most would agree with Osteen, in that he will not be the judge of anyone's eternal fate, it is, nevertheless, very telling that the leader of a congregation of over thirty thousand people (the largest in the nation), in addition to an innumerable television audience, would not stand by Jesus' very words: "*I am the way, the truth, and the life: no man cometh unto the Father, but by me*" *(John 14:6)*.

Preaching tolerance, compromise, and the *prosperity gospel*, in place of God's Word, is apostasy by its very definition. These false doctrines are currently being taught on a scale that is unparalleled.

Increase in Knowledge and Travel

But thou, O Daniel, shut up the words, and seal the book,

even to the time of the end: <u>many shall run to and fro, and knowledge shall be increased.</u>

—Daniel 12:4

This verse from the Book of Daniel suggests a dramatic increase in knowledge and travel. Both of these are significant topics, so, once again, we will examine them individually.

Knowledge:

Some believe that the reference to *"knowledge"* in this verse refers to the sum of all knowledge held by mankind at a given time, while others suggest that it speaks to an increase of knowledge and understanding of the prophecies themselves as the time of the end nears. The latter notion is supported by the command given to Daniel to *"seal the Book"* until *"the time of the end."* This refers to the fact that the prophecies in the Book of Daniel would not be fully understood until the end times.

Whichever way one chooses to interpret this passage from Daniel, it is beyond question that we have seen a literal explosion of knowledge in the twentieth century. Illustrating the point, it is a commonly cited fact that eighty to ninety percent of all scientists who have ever lived are alive today.

Further underscoring the reality, some remarks by Paul G. Kaminski, former Under Secretary of Defense for Acquisition and Technology help to put things in perspective:

"Our knowledge base is expanding at a staggering rate. While there were roughly one hundred scientific journals in 1800, there are almost 100,000 today. This knowledge explosion has not been limited to just the scientific and technical fields. It is said that mankind's knowledge has doubled between 1965 and 1990 and it will double again at the turn of the century. The president of World Trends

Research claims that "If you were to read the entire Sun-day New York Times, you would be exposed to more in-formation in that one reading than was absorbed in a lifetime by the average person living in Thomas Jeffer-son's day."[21]

Travel:

Alluding to a significant increase in travel, the angel in this verse tells Daniel that in *"the time of end: many shall run to and fro."*

To pinpoint the origins of the stunning advances in travel that we have witnessed, one need only look back a century or so to the advent of the automobile—which was soon followed by plane travel. It is mind boggling to consider that mankind went from walking, to flying, and ultimately to space travel, in the span of one generation.

It is indisputable that there has never been a greater percentage increase of either knowledge or travel in any prior generation. Moreover, it is difficult to imagine that this quantum leap could ever be equaled within the lifetime of any following generation.

A Generation Like None Other

Having examined the various ways in which the signs of the times are currently being fulfilled, one would think that even the most ardent of skeptics would be hard pressed to deny the reality that prophecy is unfolding before our eyes. Yet, despite the evidence, some contend that there is nothing unique about the times in which we live—arguing that former generations have also wit-nessed many of the same signs. These same skeptics suggest that throughout history, people have looked to various calamities that have occurred within their lifetimes in an attempt to associate them with the biblical signs of the last days.

In answer to the skeptics, many scholars have noted that there is, indeed, a major factor that distinguishes this generation from all others before it—which is, of course, the fact that we are currently witnessing the convergence of *all* of the biblical signs.

The same cannot be said for any previous generation. While there may have been periods in which mankind has experienced wars, famine, and pestilence, this would not, by any terms of measurement, indicate a fulfillment of the Scriptures.

In order for the prophecies outlined in the Books of Matthew, Daniel, Timothy, and others, to be fulfilled, the people living through the aforementioned events would also have had to experience all of the other biblical signs—including a dramatic upsurge in earthquakes and storms, a rapid proliferation of knowledge and travel, a great falling away from the faith, and finally, the gospel being preached throughout the whole world.

Conclusion

Since the time that Jesus first detailed the signs of the last days nearly two thousand years ago, the complete combination of them has never existed as it does today. Consequently, the current generation alone bears the distinction of fitting the end-times profile as described in the Bible. It is for this reason, so many are convinced that the time is near, "...*even at the doors*" *(Mark 13:29).*

We end this chapter by simply noting the instructions that Jesus gives to those who are on earth to witness these signs and who have the wisdom to recognize the times in which they live: "*And when these things begin to come to pass, then look up, and lift up your heads; for your redemption draweth nigh*" *(Luke 21:28).*

PART IV

The Role of Islam in the End Times

N ow armed with the necessary foundational knowledge with respect to both Islam and the nature of Bible prophecy, we are fully prepared to get to the heart of the matter and explore the notion of Islam as the fulfillment of the "*beast*," or "*antichrist*," that is referenced throughout the Scriptures.

We will begin by dissecting the infamous Beast of Revelation; in doing so, we will discover what this creature actually represents and how it is tied to events that are now unfolding in the Middle East.

Secondly, we thoroughly test the theory of an Islamic antichrist by applying the notion to a wide range of Scripture. Will the thesis hold up under scrutiny?

Next, we delve into both the Islamic and Christian expectations in regard to the foremost end-times figures.

And finally, we will explore the age-old enigma known as the "Mark of the beast," or "666." What is revealed will unnerve even the most dispassionate observer.

As we progress through this section, a picture should begin to emerge—one that confirms the role of Islam in the end times.

NINE

And the angel said unto me, Wherefore didst thou marvel? I will tell thee the mystery of the woman, and of the beast that carrieth her, which hath the seven heads and ten horns.

—Revelation 17:7

Decoding the End-Times Beast

Exiled to the Greek island of Patmos in the first century A.D., the Apostle John was given a vision of things to come. In this nightmarish vision, he gazed in wonder, as a beast, having *"seven heads"* and *"ten horns,"* rose from a vast sea.

As John contemplated this scene, he struggled to make sense of the strange creature before him. What was the meaning of the seven heads, and what do the horns symbolize?

In this chapter, we will answer these questions and more, as we begin to shed some much-needed light on a mystifying topic: the puzzling and somewhat bizarre *"beast"* that appears in the Book of Revelation.

A Different Type of Book

The word *revelation* means to *reveal* or *disclose*, and it is here, in the last book of the Bible, that we find Jesus Christ's disclosure of the earthly events that will culminate in His return, to establish God's Kingdom on earth.

Because of its unusual symbolic language, the Book of Revelation is difficult for many of us to read, as most are not familiar with this type of literature. This was not the case for those living in the ancient world, who would have been more accustomed to the complex nature of the writing style that we find in Revelation.

Considering that the majority of us have no experience with ancient texts, or the symbolic imagery that they often employ, we are going to briefly address the topic of symbolism and its use within the Scriptures before embarking upon our study of the "*beast.*"

Some Notes on Symbolism

The Beast that appeared in John's vision is brimming with symbolic meaning, and the Book of Revelation can, again, be utterly confounding to those who lack a basic understanding of the figurative language that it contains.

In this chapter, we will encounter such terms as "*beast,*" "*horns,*" "*seas,*" *and* "*mountains.*" While all of these words have *literal* meanings in and of themselves, they may also take on a *symbolic* meaning within the context of Revelation, as well as some other books of the Bible. In His wisdom, God has chosen the universal language of using visual symbols to communicate His visions of the future through His Prophets.

An excellent example of this symbolism is found in the following verse, in which "*sheep*" and "*mountains*" are used to represent something in a symbolic sense:

> My sheep wandered through all the mountains, and upon every high hill: yea, my flock was scattered upon all the face of the earth, and none did search or seek after them.
> —Ezekiel 34:6

When read within the context of Ezekiel 34, this verse is clearly speaking of the dispersion of the Jews from their homeland and their subsequent wanderings throughout the nations of the earth. Thus, the "*sheep*" represent the *Jewish people,* and the "*mountains*" represent the *nations of the earth.*

This type of symbolism is a common characteristic of the Book of Revelation, as well as other portions of the Bible. A general understanding of this will be helpful as we proceed.

Literal Versus Symbolic Meaning

Throughout history, many have attempted to blur the line between the literal and the symbolic language of the Bible, in effect, manipulating the meaning of the Scriptures—usually, in an effort to make them conform to a particular set of beliefs. However, the Bible should not require any creativity on the part of the reader in order to be understood, nor is its interpretation limited to any one gifted individual who is blessed with the ability to understand the prophecies. God's Word was not intended to confuse. It was meant to be understandable to anyone who diligently studies it.

Therefore, when we read a passage that is obviously employing symbolism, it should be interpreted as such. The meaning behind the symbols—assuming that it is not clearly provided in the passage—is understood by studying other Scripture, or already fulfilled prophecy, and then applying the symbolic meanings consistently throughout. A simple rule to remember is that *Scripture should be used to interpret Scripture.*

Likewise, if a passage has used *literal* terms that make perfect sense on their own, there is no need to attach symbolism to it in order to suit any particular preconceived notions. The point being that many have mistakenly attached symbolism to passages that should be interpreted literally—and vice versa.

These things being duly noted, we are now much better prepared to go forward in our search for the meaning behind the mystifying Beast of Revelation.

Looking for the Beast in all the Wrong Places

As previously noted, whether due to a simple lack of historical perspective or, perhaps, a misapplication of the symbolism, Bible scholars have, for years, been confounded by some of the more difficult prophecies—often coming to incomplete or inaccurate conclusions in regard to their meanings.

For instance, a popular theory throughout the years has been that the Antichrist Kingdom would be born of what is essentially a revived version of the Roman Empire and will most likely be led by the political and economic organization that we know as the *European Union*. For this reason, many believe that the Antichrist will be of European descent. Some even argue that he will be a Pope, or possibly a U.S. President!

The origins of the European Antichrist theory can be traced back to the widely accepted interpretations of the Book of Daniel. While space does not allow for us to delve into the biblical and historical basis that has been cited in reaching these conclusions, we will simply note the fact that was brought to light in the previous chapter, which is that the Book of Daniel itself makes it clear that the prophecies contained therein would not be fully understood until the end times: "*...seal the book, even to the time of the end*" *(Daniel 12:4)*. It thus seems likely that the long-held interpretations are destined to be incorrect or incomplete in some respect.

Nonetheless, the Roman-European antichrist theory is still predominant and has only been further advanced by the abundance of contemporary books and films depicting the last days and the rise of the Antichrist.

An example of the popular entertainment that has shaped the Western views and perceptions is, of course, the classic 1976 film, *The Omen*. After all, who could forget the spine-chilling scene in which Robert Thorn parts the hair of his sleeping son, Damien, revealing the bare scalp and a birthmark that resembles the numerals 666?

True to the traditional teachings, *The Omen*—as well as many of the more contemporary films—depict the Antichrist as being of European descent and eventually rising to power in the West. This is the notion that many in the current generation grew up with and the one that the majority of people still cling to today.

Further perpetuating the existing stereotypes, is an immensely popular fictional series that appeared on the shelves in 1995. The *Left Behind* series, by Tim LaHaye, has sold a staggering sixty-five million copies. These books presumably map out the end-times events as the author believes they will transpire. Like most of his contemporaries, LaHaye portrays the character of the Antichrist as something similar to what we see in many of the popular thrillers.

Again, as is human nature, many stubbornly resist giving up these deeply entrenched ideas—holding fast to the viewpoints that society and the media have become accustomed to.

The True Origins of the Beast Kingdom

In regard to the Antichrist, the prophecy teachers of today are, for the most part, in the same boat that the majority of Christians are in: still relying on the obsolete traditions that have been passed down through the centuries instead of looking to what the Bible actually tells us.

Even so, there are some exceptions to this general rule. It seems that due to recent world events, more and more prophecy scholars and students have begun to look toward Islam as a possible source for the Beast Kingdom that is described in the Bible.

While an Islamic Antichrist is not a completely new concept, it has most definitely not enjoyed the widespread exposure that many other theories have, and in spite of the fact that the idea is rapidly gaining momentum, it is still surprisingly unrecognized among churches and other prophecy venues. This does not come as a shock when we consider that the subject of the end times is largely ignored to begin with. And, as alluded to earlier, on the rare occasions that the topic is addressed, those speaking on it tend to stick with the teachings that they are most comfortable with.

Contrary to the conventional teachings on the end times, all of the sources used for this book look to the religion of Islam to yield the biblical figure that we refer to as the "Antichrist."

This reasoning is actually well founded in Scripture—so well founded, in fact, that many are amazed that it has escaped the notice of so many for so long. Perhaps, it is simply the proper historical perspective that was the missing ingredient.

It is with this in mind that I ask the reader to put aside all previous notions with respect to the Antichrist, as we turn to the ultimate source of enlightenment on the matter, which is, of course, the Bible.

We begin our search for the true origins of the Beast amid the passages of the Old Testament Book of Ezekiel.

The Geographic Origins of the Antichrist Kingdom

In his 2006 book, *Antichrist: Islam's Awaited Messiah*, Joel Richardson points out that one of the first major clues indicating the Islamic origins of the Beast Kingdom is found in Ezekiel 38. Here, the Prophet identifies all of the enemies that will gather against Israel in the end times.

Tellingly, each of these nations can be directly associated with a current Islamic nation. In drawing these correlations between the ancient versions and their present-day counterparts, we begin to form an accurate *geographic* picture of the Antichrist's Kingdom.

Let us take a look, then, at Ezekiel's vision of "*future years*," in which he sees many nations gathering for war:

> The word of the LORD came to me: Son of man, set your face against Gog, of the land of Magog, the chief prince of Meshech and Tubal; prophesy against him and say: 'This is what the Sovereign LORD says: I am against you, O Gog, chief prince of Meshech and Tubal. I will turn you around, put hooks in your jaws and bring you out with your whole army—your horses, your horsemen fully armed, and a great horde with large and small shields, all of them brandishing their swords. Persia, Cush and Put will be with them, all with shields and helmets, also Gomer with all its troops, and Beth Togarmah from the far north with all its troops—the many nations with you. 'Get ready; be prepared, you and all the hordes gathered about you, and take command of them. After many days you

will be called to arms. In future years you will invade a land that has recovered from war, whose people were gathered from many nations to the mountains of Israel, which had long been desolate. They had been brought out from the nations, and now all of them live in safety.

—Ezekiel 38:1-8

Before we learn the identities of these nations, we should take note of what is, perhaps, the most strikingly prophetic part of this passage, which is the startlingly clear description of modern-day Israel that we are given in the last verse. Indeed, having recovered from past wars and the dispersion, the Jews have been re-gathered to the long-desolate Promised Land and are thriving as a nation—precisely as Ezekiel predicted.

As for the enemies of Israel that Ezekiel mentions, they are, for the most part, unrecognizable to us today. They are identified as being led by "*Gog*" (referring to the Antichrist) and listed in order as *Magog, Meschech, Tubal, Persia, Cush, Put, Gomer, and Beth Togarmah.*

In our search for the modern identities of these nations, Richardson notes that seven of them are mentioned in the Book of Genesis as being the descendants of Noah and his three sons. Today, Bible scholars and historians are able to trace the names of Noah's sons to certain people groups and regions, thereby correlating them with modern nations. While the exact identification of some may be debatable, there is general agreement among scholars as to the identity of most of these peoples (Richardson, 104).

For the sake of brevity, and for our purposes here, we will not explore the details involved in making these determinations, as it is fairly involved, but will simply list the nations by their ancient versus their current names (104-109):

Magog = Asia Minor; possibly parts of Central Asia, along with some southern regions of the former Soviet Union.

Meschech = Central and western Asia Minor; portions of modern-day Turkey.

Tubal = Eastern Asia Minor; portions of modern-day Turkey.

Persia = Iran.

Cush = Sudan.

Put = Lybia.

Gomer = Central area of modern-day Turkey.

Togormah = Southeastern area of modern-day Turkey.

Having identified these nations by their modern labels, it becomes apparent that there is an emphasis on the area commonly known today as the Republic of Turkey. In fact, five of the eight nations mentioned in Ezekiel occupy various regions of Turkey, in addition to possibly the southern Russian regions near the Caucasus Mountains, as well as some of the Turkic nations of Central Asia (109).

The other three nations: Lybia, Sudan, and Iran, together with Turkey, happen to form a perfect circle around Israel. This being the case, we have no reason to believe that the final Beast Kingdom will be anything other than Islamic—unless one subscribes to the theory that these Islamic nations will eventually be overcome, or replaced, by some other type of government. While anything is possible, current trends indicate that Islam is still in the early stages of what many commentators are calling a "worldwide revival."

The Seven Headed Beast of John's Vision

Now that we have established the Islamic nature of the Antichrist's Kingdom, we refocus our attention on the principal part of our study, which is the Beast that John beheld in his vision from the Book of Revelation.

What is the meaning behind this bizarre creature, with its "*seven heads*" and "*ten horns?*" To find some answers, we begin with a verse from Revelation 13, in which John gets his first glimpse of the Beast:

> And I stood upon the sand of the sea, and saw a beast rise up out of the sea, <u>having seven heads and ten horns</u>, and upon his horns ten crowns, and upon his heads the name of blasphemy. <u>And the beast which I saw was like unto a leopard, and his feet were as the feet of a bear, and his mouth as the mouth of a lion:</u> and the dragon gave him his power, and his seat, and great authority.
>
> —Revelation 13:1, 2

This verse is teeming with information, so to avoid being overwhelmed by it we will simply approach it one piece at a time.

Beginning with the easiest part of the puzzle, we notice that the Beast gets his power and authority from the "*dragon*," which is an obvious reference to Satan. Satan's association with the dragon is established earlier in Revelation 12:7: "*And there was war in heaven: Michael and his angels fought against the dragon...*"

Notably, we see that the Beast rises out of the "*sea*." Seas or waters are used throughout the Bible to represent peoples or nations, as demonstrated in this example from Revelation 17: "*The waters which you saw, where the harlot sits, are peoples, multitudes, nations, and tongues*" *(Revelation 17:15)*. Thus, we see that this beast rises from a "*sea*" of peoples and nations.

We also learn that in addition to having multiple heads and horns, the Beast is like a "*leopard*," with the feet of a "*bear*," and the mouth of a "*lion*." It seems that the further we dig into this passage, the more confusing it becomes. However, one thing is obvious: This verse is not to be taken literally, unless we are to believe that some sort of mutated sea monster will some day rise from the ocean to attack the world!

Therefore, in order to understand what these strange animal-like attributes represent in the symbolic sense, we must employ the all-important rule that we alluded to earlier, which is to let Scripture interpret Scripture. In this case, we must go back to the Old Testament Book of Daniel.

The Books of Daniel and Revelation, though written hundreds of years apart, are considered to be inextricably intertwined, which is to say that they must be used to interpret each other, or that one cannot be fully understood apart from the other. With this understanding, a quick detour into the Book of Daniel will provide some critical insight into the Beast of Revelation.

Daniel's Beasts

In the Book of Daniel, chapter 7, we learn that Daniel *also* had a vision of some beasts, but in Daniel's vision four *"diverse"* beasts rose up out of the earth. The first of these beasts was like a lion, the second was like a bear, and the third, like a leopard. Do these animals sound familiar? They should, as they are the same creatures that make up the Beast of Revelation. Daniel's fourth beast is not likened to an animal but is described only as being *"dreadful and terrible, and strong exceedingly" (Daniel 7:7)*.

Like John from Revelation, Daniel is also confounded by the vision before him, so he asks the angel to explain the meaning of the beasts. The angel replies:

> These great beasts, which are four, are four kings, which shall arise out of the earth...Thus he said, The fourth beast shall be the fourth kingdom upon earth, which shall be diverse from all kingdoms, and shall devour the whole earth, and shall tread it down, and break it in pieces.
> —Daniel 7:17, 23

The angel makes it clear that the beasts symbolize four very great kingdoms that will come upon the world. Among Bible scholars, there is virtually unanimous agreement as to the identities of the first three kingdoms that are represented by the beasts.

In Daniel 7:4, the lion with *"eagle's wings"* is believed to represent Babylon. The winged lion was often depicted in the ancient Babylonian sculptures. Also, the Scriptures refer to Babylon as a *"lion"* in Jeremiah 4:7, and as an *"eagle"* in Ezekiel 17:3, respectively.

The bear of Daniel 7:5, with *"three ribs in the mouth of it,"* represents Medo-Persia. This Bear *"raised up itself on one side,"* which speaks of two separate components that were unequal in strength. The Medes and the Persians were both part of one empire, but the Persians became more powerful, thus raising their part of the kingdom above that of the Medes. The three ribs refer to the three main conquests of Cyrus: Lydia in 546 B.C., Egypt in 525 B.C., and Babylon in 538 B.C.

The leopard of Daniel 7:6, with *"four wings of a foul"* and *"four heads,"* represents Greece. The symbolism of a leopard with four wings alludes to the swift conquests of Alexander the Great. Many scholars also believe that this refers to his conquests of Asia Minor, Greece, Persia, and Egypt. The four heads are representative of the dividing of Alexander's Kingdom into four parts after his death.

Daniel's Fourth Beast: A Revived Rome?

As to the identity of Daniel's fourth beast, there is also unanimous agreement. It represents the final kingdom that will rule the earth before Christ's return: the Beast, or Antichrist Kingdom.

Again, the widely held belief down through the centuries has been that this fourth beast would originate from the old Roman Empire. Considering the fact that the Roman Empire has long since vanished, the "Roman" theorists believe that it must be *revived* in order to fulfill its role as the antichrist power. This means that today's Europe would, in essence, have to transform itself into the *devouring* beast that we see described in Daniel: *"...and it had great iron teeth: it devoured and brake in pieces, and stamped the residue with the feet of it" (Daniel 7:7).*

To say that this description is not in line with the general disposition of most European countries today would be an understatement. The reality is that most of the European nations are currently much more inclined to *appease* their enemies than they are to "*tread*" them down or to "*devour*" them as we see the Antichrist Kingdom doing. And while anything is possible, there is a much more realistic possibility, which involves an empire that has risen since the fall of the Roman Empire.

The More likely Suspect

Considering today's political landscape, an Islamic Empire in the role of Daniel's fourth beast (the Antichrist Kingdom) appears to be a likely possibility. Nevertheless, for something so central to our thesis, a mere hunch based on the current reality is not enough to build a solid case upon.

Fortunately, we also have strong biblical support for this notion, namely in that all three of the other beasts from Daniel, which represent the kingdoms of Babylon, Persia, and Greece, inhabited the same specific region of the Middle East. Once again, the Roman Empire does not seem to fit, as it points more or less to European geography. It is much more logical to conclude that the fourth Beast Kingdom would occupy the same region as the first three beasts. The Islamic Empire of the past, as well as the Islamic nations of the present, certainly fit this criterion. In light of this, common sense dictates that the fourth beast will be Islamic.

Back to the Beast of Revelation

Now that we have identified the origins of Daniel's beasts, let us refocus our attention on the Beast of Revelation, while acknowledging that our study of Daniel's beasts has given us a necessary point of reference from which to interpret the leopard, bear, and lion aspects of Revelation's beast.

Notably, the Beast of Revelation appears to be a composite of Daniel's separate beasts, which, again, represent Babylon, Persia, and Greece. This is a critical piece of information in that it indicates shared geographic (Middle Eastern) origins with Daniel's beasts. Thus, it is only with the clues provided in the Book of Daniel that we have been able to determine the true geographic—and ultimately Islamic—origins of the Beast of Revelation.

Again, the insight gained from Daniel underscores the point made earlier, which is that the Books of Daniel and Revelation cannot be fully understood apart from each other.

What are the Seven Heads of the Beast?

Having solved the puzzle presented by the *body* of the Beast of Revelation, we must now determine the meaning of the "*heads*."

In search of an answer to this part of the mystery, we look to Revelation 17:

> And here is the mind which hath wisdom. <u>The seven heads are seven mountains</u>, on which the woman sitteth.
> —Revelation 17:9

This verse plainly states that the "*seven heads*" represent "*seven mountains*." As we learned earlier, in our discussion pertaining to symbolism in the Bible, *mountains* commonly represent *nations* or *kingdoms*. Therefore, each of the seven heads represents a separate kingdom.

We also note the fact that all seven heads, or *kingdoms*, are joined together on the body of one beast (Revelation 13:1). This indicates that these kingdoms all share a characteristic or quality that unites them. To be sure, these kingdoms must have something very significant in common—but what could it be?

By carefully studying the Bible and, also, the history of the Middle East, we are able to single out a specific trait that is shared among seven kingdoms that have ruled in the region. This trait links these kingdoms in an obvious manner, serving to identify them as the seven heads of the Beast.[1]

Significantly, this shared attribute appears to be an occupation of Jerusalem, which is, of course, the capitol of Israel. Indeed, throughout the course of history, each of the seven kingdoms—which are represented by the heads of the Beast—has ruled over, or occupied, the Holy City of Jerusalem.

In considering the occupation of Jerusalem as the unifying factor among the seven kingdoms, it is essential to bear in mind a fact that was brought to light in earlier chapters: The Bible is very *Israel centric* and primarily describes events taking place exclusively in the Holy Land and surrounding areas. While this concept may seem strange to some, it actually makes perfect sense when one considers that Jerusalem is the capitol city of the land given by God exclusively to the Jewish people. It was also, of course, the dwelling place of the Ark of the Covenant, which, at the time, was representative of the singular physical manifestation of God's presence on earth.

It stands to reason that for any foreign kingdom to occupy this land—after God had given it to the Jews—would be in direct opposition to the covenant that He made with Abraham. Accordingly, we should not be surprised that the occupation of Jerusalem, specifically, is the distinguishing factor that identifies a kingdom as one of the heads of the Beast.

The Identities of the Seven Kingdoms Revealed

The next step in understanding the Beast of Revelation is to identify *which* kingdoms are represented by each of the seven heads.

The task of identifying the kingdoms, or heads, that have ruled over Jerusalem is a fairly straightforward one. It is essentially a matter of examining the historical data. Although, there is still room for error—as some scholars have proven—by not recognizing certain defining criteria when determining the identities of the seven kingdoms.

For instance, some have included Egypt among the seven, but the Egyptians have never occupied Jerusalem. In the fifteenth century B.C., they did, in fact, rule over the region when it was known as Canaan, but this was before Jerusalem existed, or was *inherited* by the Jews.[2] The historical record reveals that Jerusalem was not established by King David until 1000 B.C.; for this reason, Egypt is excluded as a head of the beast.

Some have also included Assyria as one of the seven kingdoms, but this too is incorrect. While the Assyrians did conquer the Northern Kingdom of Israel, they never took Jerusalem.[3] Again, the key distinction that many have missed is that the kingdom—in order to qualify as one of the seven heads—had to occupy Jerusalem at some point.

On this same topic, some would question the absence of the *Crusaders* of medieval times from the list of seven kingdoms, as they, indeed, occupied Jerusalem for a time when they recaptured it from the Muslims in 1099 A.D. Though the Crusaders did conquer Jerusalem, they are not included among the seven heads of the Beast because they were not a *kingdom*, or an *empire*. The Crusades were essentially an international effort organized by the Pope to re-claim the Holy Lands from the Barbarian Turks.[4] Consequently, the Crusaders do not meet the requirement of being a *major kingdom* that occupied Jerusalem.

Having noted these important qualifiers, we have eliminated the possibility of making the same errors that many others have made in their interpretations.

As we move one step closer to solving the puzzle, we read on from Revelation 17 for further clues:

> There are also <u>seven kings. Five have fallen, one is, and the other has not yet come</u>. And when he comes, he must continue a short time.
>
> —Revelation 17:10

We learn from this verse that there are also seven *"kings"* that correlate to the seven *"kingdoms."* Assuming our theory to be correct, the seven kings mentioned here represent seven kingdoms that have, at one time, occupied Jerusalem.

The verse also tells us that five of the kings *"have fallen"* and that one is *"not yet come."* This indicates that the kings ruled in succession, or one after the other. It does not mean that five had fallen at John's time, which is another point that is often overlooked. John is seeing this vision from a point of view far in the future, *not from his present day (first century) time period.*[8]

Now, as we take into consideration all of the above, we are finally prepared to identify the seven kingdoms that are represented by the seven heads of the Beast.

Starting with Babylon, the seven empires that have ruled in the Middle East, North Africa, and Southern Europe, but specifically Jerusalem, are as follows:

1 - Babylonian
2 - Media-Persian
3 - Greek
4 - Roman
5 - Arabic
6 - Ottoman
7 - British

Note that the fifth and sixth kingdoms—although both Islamic—are listed separately. Some scholars have mistakenly combined the Arabic and Ottoman empires into one "Islamic Empire." This, along with the other common errors that were mentioned earlier, has led some to conclude that the seventh head of the Beast was *Islamic* rather than the British Empire.

History reveals that the Arabic empire, started by Muhammed in 632 A.D., lasted for approximately six hundred years. The Ottoman Empire began in 1299, and although Islamic, it was not Arabic.

This common oversight leads to a faulty interpretation of the identities of the seven heads.

The Seventh Head of the Beast

To further bolster the validity of our list of seven kingdoms, or heads of the Beast, we consider an important clue that we are given in Revelation 17:10 regarding the identity of the seventh head: "*And when he comes, he must continue a short time.*"

This passage makes it clear that the seventh kingdom will only rule over Jerusalem for a "*short time.*" Thus, in order for a kingdom to be validated as the seventh, it must meet this requirement.

History tells us that the British Empire was the last empire to control Jerusalem before the Jews regained control of the land. In order to confirm the notion that the British Empire is, indeed, the seventh head of the Beast, we need only verify that it ruled over Jerusalem for a "*short time*" relative to the others on the list.[5]

The Short Rule of the British Empire

The British took Jerusalem from The Ottomans during World War One in December of 1917 and ruled it until Israel became an independent nation again in 1948. True to the word of the Bible, the British occupation of the Holy City was, by far, the shortest in duration (only thirty-one years) relative to the other candidates. Therefore, the British Empire alone fits the profile of the seventh king that would continue for "*a short time.*"[6]

The British Empire gradually gave independence to most of its subject nations during the twentieth century—as a result, ceasing to be an empire itself. Currently, there are no empires left in the world, as even the Soviet Empire has disintegrated.

Now that we understand the meaning behind the *body* and the "*heads*" of the Beast, we take a look at the "*horns,*" as we move yet another step closer to solving this puzzle.[7]

A Kingdom Unique From the Others

A commonly held misconception is that the seventh head of the beast will be the last and final head, or kingdom. Clearly, this is not the case, as Revelation 17 describes an "*eighth*" head. However, the Bible tells us that there will be something very unusual about this eighth kingdom. It will, in fact, be distinct from the other seven in an obvious way. Though, in order to appreciate the unique nature of this eighth and last kingdom, we must first address the "*ten horns*" of the Beast that John saw in his vision.

In Revelation 17, John is taken away into the "*wilderness*" and given an up-close vision of the final, or "*eighth*," head, which is to be the last ruling (Antichrist) kingdom whose sole purpose is to persecute God's people on earth:[10]

> So he carried me away in the spirit into the wilderness: and I saw a woman sit upon a scarlet colored beast, full of names of blasphemy, having seven heads and <u>ten horns</u>.
> —Revelation 17:3

The woman who sits upon the Beast is another fascinating aspect of this prophecy, about which another smaller book could be written, yet she is not critical to our understanding of the Beast itself. This being the case, for the sake of both clarity and brevity, this woman's identity will not be explored here. For now, we simply note that the Beast has "*ten horns*." The angel later explains to John the meaning of these horns:

> <u>And the ten horns which thou sawest are ten kings</u>, which have received no kingdom as yet; but receive power as kings one hour with the beast. <u>These have one mind, and shall give their power and strength unto the beast.</u> These shall make war with the Lamb, and the Lamb shall overcome them: for he is Lord of lords, and King of kings: and they that are with him are called, and chosen, and

faithful…<u>For God hath put in their hearts to fulfill his will, and to agree, and give their kingdom unto the beast,</u> until the words of God shall be fulfilled.

—Revelation 17:12-14, 17

It is revealed to John that each horn represents a king, each of which will receive power for "*one hour*" (a short time) by agreeing to give their "*power and strength*" to the Beast. Apparently, the eighth kingdom will be the result of a decision made by ten kings to unite as one.

The Eighth Head: The Final Beast Kingdom

By combining their strength, the ten "*horns*," or "*kings*," will form an extremely powerful empire. The fact that this empire is an amalgamation of ten smaller nations and will only exist for a short time distinguishes it from the other seven kingdoms, or heads, that came before it. The sole purpose of this kingdom is to "*make war*" against the "*Lamb*" (Christ) and to exercise the power of the "*beast*" (Satan) over all of the earth.

With this in mind, we again return to Revelation 17, where we learn yet more about the identity of the eighth head of the Beast:

> The beast that thou sawest was, and is not; and shall ascend out of the bottomless pit, and go into perdition: and they that dwell on the earth shall wonder, whose names were not written in the book of life from the foundation of the world, when they behold the beast that <u>was, and is not, and yet is</u>…And the beast that <u>was, and is not, even he is the eighth,</u> and is of the seven, and goeth into perdition.
>
> —Revelation 17:8, 11

At first glance, the word play in this passage may seem confusing, but if one takes the time to study what these two verses are actually saying, it becomes quite clear.

The line describing the Beast that *"was, and is not, and yet is"* speaks to the fact that the Beast Kingdom existed previously as one of the seven. Then, for a period of time it does not exist. Finally, it will re-emerge in a revived state. In other words, one of the former seven heads, or kingdoms, will come back to fulfill the role of the eighth and final.

But which empire will it be? Revelation 13 provides an important clue:

> And I saw one of his heads as it were wounded to death; and his deadly wound was healed: and all the world wondered after the beast.
>
> —Revelation 13:3

This verse tells us that at some point one of the heads, or kingdoms, is *"wounded to death"* and, therefore, ceases to exist. Then, in the second line, we see that the *"wound was healed"* and the Beast returns—to the amazement of many—as the eighth and last kingdom. Significantly, this description of the revival of the wounded head correlates precisely with Revelation 17 and the head that *"was, and is not, and yet is."*

In order to identify which of the seven will be *"healed"* and return as the Beast Kingdom, it is simply a matter of consulting history to determine which of the seven empires was *"wounded to death."* The Beast Kingdom will not be a kingdom that simply fell apart like the Arabic empire or dissolved itself like the British Empire. The Beast Kingdom was *killed* in warfare. When it comes back to life the world will be stunned, as it will have been quite some time since it had received its fatal wound, and typically, when an empire falls there is no coming back.

A Revived Islamic Ottoman Empire

The Ottoman Empire, under the rule of the Caliphs, was built on the scrapes of the Arabic and Roman Empires and was one of the most powerful states in the world during the fifteenth and six-teenth centuries. It lasted for more than six hundred years before being defeated, or *"wounded to death,"* by the Allied forces in 1922.[11]

As we learned in previous chapters, the history of the Islamic Empire—including both the Arab and Ottoman periods—was one of almost constant bloody warfare, much of it directed toward Jews and Christians.

If our thesis is correct, the end-times Beast Kingdom that is referenced throughout the Bible will be a revived version of the Is-lamic Ottoman Empire. The exception being that this new incarna-tion will be even more formidable than the former.

The Seat of the Beast

Now that the end-times Beast Kingdom has been unmasked as a revived version of the Islamic Ottoman Empire, a point of utmost importance should be made:

As referenced in chapter six, when the Ottoman Empire was *"wounded to death"* in the early part of the twentieth century—resulting in the fall of the Caliphate—it was replaced by the Turk-ish Republic and various successor states in southeastern Europe and the Middle East. Bearing this in mind, we refer back to the be-ginning of this chapter, recalling that the geographic region known as modern-day Turkey figures prominently among the coalition of nations that Ezekiel identifies as the Antichrist's kingdom. Thus, Turkey's apparent involvement in the coalition that attacks Israel meshes precisely with our thesis that assumes a revived Ottoman Empire as the Beast Kingdom. In fact, the Republic of Turkey oc-cupies the region once known as the very *seat* of the Ottoman Em-pire!

It is interesting to note that when the Islamic Ottomans were conquered and absorbed by the newly formed Turkish Republic their national flag did not change. It remains, today, the crescent moon and star on a solid background of scarlet. While most likely a matter of pure coincidence, we find an eerie correlation with the color of the Beast from John's vision. Revelation 17:3 confirms that it is also scarlet: "...*and I saw a woman sit upon a scarlet coloured beast, full of names of blasphemy, having seven heads and ten horns.*"[12]

The Purpose of the Beast

All throughout history, the satanically inspired empires that are represented by the seven heads of the Beast have served a common purpose, which has been to make war. For some, it was solely to plunder other nations. In the case of the Greeks, it was to spread Hellenistic culture. Though, there is only one reason that the next, and last, beast will come to power, and that is to conquer the world for Islam.[13]

According to what is written in the Bible, it appears that the Beast Kingdom will attempt to do just that. Revelation 13:4 speaks of an empire so fierce that it inspires willful submission among those who would stand against it. In those days, many will say, "...*Who is like unto the beast? who is able to make war with him?*"

Summary and Conclusions

In this chapter, using both Scripture and historical data, we have effectively dissected the Beast of Revelation. We have also revealed the geographic (Middle Eastern) origins of the final Beast Kingdom and identified one nation that is of particular interest, which will be further explored in the following chapter.

Perhaps most importantly, we have learned that this final kingdom will be a revived version of one that has previously existed: the Ottoman Empire. This Kingdom will be the by-product of ten "*kings,*" or rulers, who agree to combine their wealth, weaponry, and manpower for the cause of Islam. Indeed, the world will be amazed at the rebirth of an Islamic Empire.

TEN

INSTANBUL, Feb. 9, 2008: Turkey's parliament voted Saturday to end a more than eighty year old ban on women wearing (Islamic) head scarves at universities, acknowledging the rising influence of conservative Islam in the most determinedly secular republic of the Muslim world.

— Washington Post Foreign Service

The Awakening of the Beast

When Mustafa Kemal Ataturk founded the Republic of Turkey, on October 29, 1923, he led his country into a new era of peace and stability. As part of his reforms, he implemented a new civil law code and abolished the religious courts and schools. The official day of rest was changed from Friday—which is the Muslim holy day—to Sunday. The Western solar calendar was also adopted in lieu of the Islamic calendar.

Turning his back on the Islamic past of the fallen Ottoman Empire, Ataturk established Turkey under the redesigned foreign policy motto of, *"Peace at home, peace in the world."*

Today, nearly eighty-five years later, Turkey presumably remains a secular country—despite the fact that ninety-eight percent of its population profess to be Muslim.

Is Change Coming to Turkey?

In light of Turkey's historically peaceful posture, is it possible that this nation could join with others in the region and morph into the devouring *"beast"* with *"great iron teeth"* that the Bible predicts? Will this nation, in fact, play a pivotal role in the revived Islamic Empire that will wreak havoc in the Middle East, bringing about a time of global chaos?

Given its staunch secular heritage, one would think that of all the Islamic countries, Turkey would be the least likely of suspects. However, it is this very notion that makes what is currently taking place within Turkey so very interesting.

In recent years, the winds of change have begun to blow across the Turkish Republic. Commentators have noted an apparent shift away from the staunchly secular ideals of Turkey's founder and toward the Islamic heritage of the Ottoman Empire.

While some of these changes may appeal to the majority Muslim population, many observers—including some secular Turks—view them with a sense of foreboding. Could it be that the Islamic head of the beast has merely been playing dead for the past eighty-five years?

A Shift in Attitude

The Iraq War has proven to be an ongoing point of contention between the U.S. and Turkey. In 2003, at the very onset of the war, the Turkish republic voted *not* to allow American forces to use Turkey as a staging ground to attack Saddam Hussein's regime.[1] This refusal bred mutual suspicion between the Turks and the U.S.—who have historically been allies—and was, perhaps, just the beginning of more overt policy shifts in which Turkey would begin to emphasize relations with its Arab neighbors and lessen its dependence on the West.

What is more, suspicions of a growing anti-American sentiment in Turkey have only been heightened by a June 2007 Pew Research Center survey, which found that only nine percent of Turkish citizens have a favorable opinion of the United States.[2] This is the lowest percentage rating of all forty-seven countries surveyed—including the virulently anti-American Palestinian territories.

Turkey's First Islamic President

In late summer of 2007, Turkey elected Abdullah Gul as its first ever president with a background in political Islam.

Gul's first bid for president was sidetracked six months prior, when secular parliamentarians boycotted the session that was set for the election of a president. Mass demonstrations were staged by secularists and women who feared that the election of a Muslim to the presidency would open the door to an *Islamified* government and, in turn, the demise of their liberal lifestyle.[3] In spite of all this, a later appeal for general elections by AKP party leader, Prime Minister Recep Tayyip Erdogan, led to a victory for Gul the second time around—thus, securing his position as the first Muslim ever elected to the Office of the President in Turkey.

The Return of Islamic Headscarves: Fashion Trend of the Future?

A mere six months after Gul took office, as if to validate the fears of many women and secularists in Turkey, the long-standing ban on wearing the traditional Muslim head scarf in public offices and universities was lifted.

Significantly, the military had no immediate objection to the lift of the ban, which was put in place by Ataturk in the 1920s. This is noteworthy, as throughout Turkey's eighty-five year history the military has been viewed as the guardian and defender of the founder's staunch secular vision of government. To be sure, the Turkish government has, since its inception, been determined to stave off any Islamic influence.[4]

Nonetheless, in comments referencing the lifting of the ban, Tanju Tosun, a political analyst at Ege University in the city of Ismir, noted the following: "...*unfortunately there is a growing trend of Islamic movements in Turkey,*"..."*The military has no choice—it must accept this result.*"[5]

Rejected by the West?

Another piece of the puzzle with respect to the future of Turkey is the nation's long-standing goal of being admitted to the European Union. Turkey has been trying to become a member of the EU since 1959, when it was still known as the European Economic Community.

In more recent years, President Gul has been credited with further carrying the torch by relentlessly pursuing Turkey's goal of joining the EU; although, currently it appears that Turkey may again be frustrated in their attempts. If Europe goes along with French President Sarkozy's aim of downgrading Turkey's possible membership in the EU to that of *privileged partnership*, the Turks may be tempted to look elsewhere.[6]

Hugh Pope, author of *Sons of the Conquerors: The Rise of the Turkic World*, and a senior analyst at the influential International Crisis Group, says downgrading Turkey's EU ambition *"would amount to a discriminatory slap in the face."* He further writes:[7]

> *"Turks will take it as more evidence that the West cannot conceive of equality with Muslims. The wider Islamic world, which is closely following EU treatment of what is arguably the most democratic, secular and successful Muslim state, will draw the same conclusion."*[8]

Descent into Islam

Heightening the concerns of many observers, the pro-Israel Washington Institute for Near East Policy, which had always praised Turkey—presumably because of its friendly ties with Israel—has recently distributed a scathing critique of the nation by its director of the Turkish Research Program.

In an article that was carried in the September 2007 edition of "Newsweek," Soner Cagaptayhe is quoted as saying:

> *"Turkey will become a more Islamic society in its foreign-policy outlook and culture. Anti-Western sentiments will grow. Headscarves, religious education and the rejection of alcohol will become more common. The Turkey of old will slowly disappear, leaving in its place a profoundly different—and potentially much more unstable—nation."*[9]

A New Role in the Region

In yet another peculiar twist, according to an article from the "Jewish Global News Service," it has been widely noted among Middle East commentators that Turkey now appears to be re-posturing itself diplomatically in the region.

In early November of 2007, both the Israeli and Palestinian Authority Presidents addressed the Turkish Parliament, marking the *first time an Israeli head of state has spoken in the legislature of a Muslim country*. Just days before that, Saudi Arabia's King Abdullah was in town for what was, notably, only the second visit to Turkey by a monarch in the last forty years. That trip came just a few weeks after an official visit to Ankara (Turkey's capitol) by Bashar Assad. This marks the *first time ever* that a Syrian president has come to Turkey.

Many Middle East observers acknowledge that all of this would have been nearly inconceivable only a few years ago.[10] For decades, Turkey has kept the Arab and Muslim countries of the Middle East at arm's length as it focused on cementing its alliance with the West and distancing itself from the Ottoman Empire's Islamic past.[11] Now, however, in what some are characterizing as a complete reversal of political posture, Turkey is making an effort to strengthen ties with its Arab neighbors, while, at the same time, recasting itself in a new role—that of a mediator, or peace broker, in the region.

Notably, in his speech to the five hundred and fifty member parliament in Ankara, Israeli President, Shimon Peres, suggested that Turkey's growing regional involvement gives it a part to play in helping to solve the Middle East conflict. Indeed, Peres' suggestion alludes to some very interesting and perhaps game changing developments in the Middle East.

A New Hope for Peace?

In March of 2008, Syrian President, Bashar Assad, confirmed that he has been holding high-level talks with Israel's Prime minister,

Ehud Olmert. The recent talks center on renewing negotiations over an Israeli retreat from the Golan Heights, which is a strategic mountainous territory that overlooks Israeli and Syrian population centers.[12]

Top diplomatic sources in Jerusalem report that Defense Minister, Ehud Barak, has been passing official messages on a regular basis to Syrian President, Assad—via Turkish mediators—with the sanctioning of Turkish President, Abdullah Gul.[13] In describing Turkey's role in the negotiations, Syrian Foreign Ministry spokeswoman, Bushra Kanfani, told a Kuwaiti newspaper, *"Turkey is used as a channel of communication"* and *"listens to both sides' positions."*[14]

Many who hear the seemingly positive news of Turkey's burgeoning role as a peace broker will find encouragement in the idea that a nation—other than the U.S.—is actively participating in the improvement of relations between Israel and her Arab neighbors.

On the other hand, those who subscribe to the notion that Turkey will play a significant role in the Beast Kingdom tend to view these gestures more with a sense of apprehension than of hope. So, why the uneasiness, you ask?

"and by peace shall destroy many..."

In the previous chapter, which explored the origins of the Beast Kingdom, we focused primarily on the *conquering* nature of the Antichrist—recalling the image of Daniel's *"dreadful and terrible"* beast, as well as Ezekiel's description of the Islamic coalition that surrounds Israel in the end times. Yet, it is perhaps even more important to understand that according to the Bible the Antichrist will, at first, emerge onto the scene as a *peacemaker*. In fact, it will initially appear to many that he is resolving conflict and brokering peace in the Middle East. This is a critical point, as it is given much emphasis in the Scriptures. Specifically, we find multiple references to the deceptively peaceful demeanor of the Antichrist in the Book of Daniel:

And through his policy also he shall cause craft to prosper in his hand; and he shall magnify himself in his heart, <u>and by peace shall destroy many:</u> he shall also stand up against the Prince of princes; but he shall be broken without hand.

—Daniel 8:25

And in his estate shall stand up a vile person, to whom they shall not give the honour of the kingdom: <u>but he shall come in peaceably, and obtain the kingdom by flatteries.</u> And with the arms of a flood shall they be overflown from before him, and shall be broken; yea, also <u>the prince of the covenant. And after the league made with him he shall work deceitfully</u>: for he shall come up, and shall become strong with a small people. <u>He shall enter peaceably even upon the fattest places of the province;</u> and he shall do that which his fathers have not done, nor his fathers' fathers; he shall scatter among them the prey, and spoil, and riches: yea, and he shall forecast his devices against the strong holds, even for a time.

—Daniel 11:21-24

These verses underscore the fact that the Antichrist will operate under the guise of *"peace"* to obtain his true objective, which is the complete and utter destruction of Israel.

Obviously, viewing these verses in light of Turkey's new role as a mediator in the region, certain questions come to mind.

Will the Antichrist Come From Turkey?

Having noted the uncanny parallel between Turkey's current political posture and the Antichrist's initial peaceful conduct, it should be emphasized that while we have clearly identified the Nation of Turkey as a prominent player in the Antichrist's coalition, we cannot be certain that the individual who will be recognized as the Antichrist actually comes from Turkey. There are some prophecy scholars who actually believe that he will hail from Syria. We find biblical support for this notion in various places; the most obvious example being the Book of Isaiah, in which the Antichrist is repeatedly referred to as *"the Assyrian."*

Nonetheless, based solely on Scripture, a convincing argument could be made for either Turkey or Syria as the country of origin for the "peace maker" that Christians will know as the Antichrist. The remarkable thing to note here is that we find the two "prime suspects" currently involved in peace negotiations with Israel: Syria as the partner in peace and Turkey as the mediator! Needless to say, these developments are being watched very closely by many of those who study Bible prophecy.

Summary and Conclusions

For the first time in history, events in the Middle East seem to be falling into perfect alignment with what the Scriptures predict toward the end of the age. Turkey, once the seat of the mighty Ottoman Empire, has just elected its first Islamic President. Many analysts believe that President Gul is already making moves to lead the country back in the direction of its Islamic past and that, likewise, the growing trend of Islamism within the secular government will continue.

There has also been a notable cooling in U.S.-Turkish relations, as Turkey reaches out to its Arab neighbors. This shift in attitude essentially amounts to a reversal of the Turkish foreign policy of the past.

Further, in establishing closer ties with its Middle Eastern neighbors, Turkey has begun to posture itself as a peace broker in the region, which some find alarming in light of the thesis put forth here.

Considering the magnitude of the recent changes in Turkey, combined with the fact that they have all occurred within an extremely short period of time, one is left to wonder whether we are witnessing an astonishing string of coincidences or if, perhaps, the Bible prophecies are playing out right before our eyes.

Could these latest events be signaling changes that will result in a nation no longer an ally to the United States? Will Turkey's frustration with its, so far, unsuccessful negotiations to become a member of the E.U. eventually lead them to look elsewhere—possibly to a future Islamic Union?

As things continue to unfold, the picture that is forming takes on a surreal quality, as the line between the current reality and the ancient Bible prophecies becomes increasingly blurred.

At this point, it is impossible to tell if the ongoing transformation in Turkey will culminate in a decision by its ruler to unite with nine other kings, or "*horns*," in the region—thereby forming a new Islamic Empire, or Caliphate. Though, it is certain that when this does happen, you will be counted among those discerning individuals who recognize this newly formed coalition as the fulfillment of the eighth head of the Beast—the Antichrist Kingdom.

ELEVEN

Test everything. Hold on to the good.

—1 Thessalonians 5:21

Testing the Theory

A popular story claims that one of the foremost intellects of all time, Isaac Newton, was inspired to formulate his theory of universal gravitation by the fall of an apple from a tree. Cartoons have gone further, to suggest that the apple actually hit Newton on the head and that its impact somehow made him aware of the force of gravity.

As Isaac Newton might have attested to, often times the keys to life's most difficult puzzles are hanging just out of our field of vision—perhaps within reach, but still unrecognized—until they drop like an apple from a tree and hit us on the head. Suddenly, the missing piece has fallen into place and the proverbial light bulb has been turned on, illuminating the solution to the entire puzzle.

In regard to Bible prophecy, many are coming to believe that Islam is that missing piece, and the rise in global terrorism is, in many ways, the apple that has fallen.

A Key to Understanding

Throughout the millennia, Bible scholars have labored to grasp the meaning behind some of the more mysterious passages of Scripture. Many have struggled in vain, however, lacking the necessary insight to unlock the mysteries contained therein.

In identifying Islam as the end-times Beast, we have established a paradigm, or a *model*, against which we can compare various end-times passages from the Books of Daniel, Revelation and others. This model can thus be used to test the viability of our theory across a broad range of Scripture.

In this chapter, we will put to full use our knowledge of Islamic behaviors and principles by holding these things up to what the Bible tells us about the Antichrist. Will our *Islamic* insight cast a revealing light on the end-times prophecies, or will they remain shrouded in mystery?

Considering the laws of chance and probability—and also allowing for the fertile imaginations of some who study prophecy—it would not be unrealistic to assume that one might find several verses which seem to harmonize with the concept of an Islamic Antichrist. Nevertheless, in order to be considered viable, the Islamic antichrist model must fit squarely with what the Bible says, not only in one or two instances but in *every* regard; if it does not, the theory must be rejected.

Testing the Theory

In order to test our theory, we will begin by taking a look at some well-known yet consistently perplexing verses. For the purposes of this exercise, keep in mind that, as we learned in chapter nine, the term *"beast"* generally refers to a *kingdom*, within the context of Bible symbolism. Therefore, since we are proposing that Islam is the Antichrist power of the end times, we will mentally assign *Islam*, or an *Islamic kingdom*, to the term *"beast"* where it is used in the Scriptures.

Having noted this, let us start the ball rolling by examining our first test subject: a verse from Revelation 13, in which we are introduced to a mysterious *"image."*

An Image to the Beast

And deceiveth them that dwell on the earth by the means of those miracles which he had power to do in the sight of the beast; <u>saying to them that dwell on the earth, that they should make an image to the beast,</u> which had the wound by a sword, and did live.

—Revelation 13:14

160

In this verse, we find ourselves witness to, perhaps, one of the Antichrist's most significant actions in the last days. Specifically, we observe that he is telling *"them that dwell on the earth"* to *"make an image to the beast."*

Until recently, most Bible scholars have had no plausible explanation for the meaning of this *"image."* Some have suggested that it might be a statue, or an idol, of some kind. Though, if we assume the image to be some type of idol, or inanimate object, we are faced with a dilemma in that the Antichrist later causes many to *"worship"* the image (Revelation 13:15). If they refuse to worship the image, he orders that they should be killed. This obviously presents a problem for the Islamic antichrist thesis, as a true Muslim would not, under any circumstance, wittingly bow to worship an object or idol. As noted throughout this book, the very foundation of Islam is based on the notion that Allah is the one and only god. This being the case, for the Antichrist to propose that anyone bow before a graven image of any kind would make him guilty of an unpardonable sin from the Islamic perspective.

Considering this, if our Islamic Antichrist theory is to pass the test, there must be some other explanation for this "image"—but what could it be?

To gain some insight into the intended meaning of this verse, we are going to focus on the key word, which is, of course, *"image."* In this case, it will be helpful to look at the way in which the word *image* is used elsewhere in the Bible. For instance, in the Book of Genesis we note that God uses it thusly: *"Let Us make man in Our image, according to Our likeness..." (Genesis 1:26).* Here, God is essentially saying that man was created as an animate, flesh and blood *"likeness"* of Himself. If we apply this same concept to our verse from the Book of Revelation and think of this *"image"* as more of a living, breathing imitation, or *likeness*, of something—rather than a mere object—the verse takes on a slightly different flavor. It now seems to suggest that this individual (the Antichrist) is not calling on those who dwell on the earth to make a statue, or an idol, in tribute to the *"beast"* but is, instead, calling on them to *assume a likeness*, or to imitate the Beast—in effect, making a copy of *Islam*. In other words, the Antichrist is saying to all nations that they should model their societies into a likeness of Islamic society—a society based on Islamic laws and principles, or *Sharia*.

In putting out the call to Islam, the Antichrist is echoing the frequent statements made by Osama bin laden and other prominent Muslim leaders of today. Indeed, like his fellow Muslims, the Antichrist desires that the entire world be modeled in the ideal *"image"* of Islam.

It is amazing to consider that this verse may very well be alluding to the recent—and future—call for the re-establishment of an Islamic Caliphate, which would, of course, be modeled after the image of the Arab and Ottoman Empires of the past. Today, there is only one world religion or political ideology on earth that wishes to impose its own laws and principles on all people, thereby forcing all nations to remake themselves in its own image. It is Islam.

The Image "Speaks"

And he had power to <u>give life unto the image </u>of the beast, that the image of the beast should both speak, <u>and cause that as many as would not worship the image of the beast should be killed</u>.

—Revelation 13:15

In the previous verse, we observed the Antichrist putting out the call to *"make an image to the beast."* Here we see that he somehow has the *"power"* to *"give life unto the image"*—and then he causes all who *"would not worship"* the image to *"be killed."* Again, this verse has been found by many a scholar to be utterly bewildering. Though, as it happens, our Islamic insight may serve to dispel some of the mystery.

Having established that the *"image to the beast"* is likely a *new* Islamic Empire—which has been modeled after the former Islamic

Empire—one might reasonably conclude that the implied meaning behind giving "*life unto the image*" refers to the Antichrist using his "*power*," or worldly influence, to symbolically "*give life*" to his newly formed kingdom. Assuming this to be the case, the verse goes on to tell us that the "*image to the beast*," or new Islamic Empire, now has the power to "*speak*" with authority and order that those who do not worship the "*beast*" (Islam) "*should be killed.*"

It should be noted that in ascribing a symbolic meaning to the Antichrist's giving "*life unto the image*," we have not merely made an arbitrary decision to do so. As we learned earlier, the Book of Revelation is, for the most part, a symbolic book, in which allegory is used to illustrate literal events. Therefore, the imagery of the Antichrist *symbolically* giving life to the Beast (Islam) fits very well within the overall genre of the Book. Further, the alternative possibility—which is to interpret this verse *literally*—presumes that the Antichrist (or Satan) actually has the power to give life to some type of inanimate image or statue. This, of course, is not a plausible interpretation, as only God has the power to give life.

At this point, having analyzed only two verses, we can already see a picture beginning to form: The Antichrist has essentially ordered all those who dwell on the earth to create a *new* Islamic Empire, or Caliphate. As we witness the birth of this kingdom, it becomes increasingly clear that the Antichrist is a ruler who wishes to impose a specific set of laws and principles upon all those who "*dwell on the earth.*" By telling all to assume a likeness of the Beast, he is, in all reality, requiring that everyone convert to Islam and submit to Islamic Laws. The only alternative for those who do not, is death.

Again, this model of behavior fits squarely with Islamic beliefs and ideals. These same actions can be consistently observed in the headlines today, as Islamic extremists call for the entire world to be ruled under Islam and Sharia Law. All dedicated Muslims who follow the teachings of the Koran are commanded to advance Islam until it is the only religion. Simply put, the goal of Islam is to rule the world.

No Regard for the Gods of His Fathers—or for the Desire of Women

In the following verse from the Book of Daniel, we observe yet more telling behavior on the part of the Antichrist. His actions and conduct serve to expose the underpinnings of his belief system:

> Neither shall he regard the gods of his fathers, nor the desire of women, nor regard any god; for he shall magnify himself above all.
>
> —Daniel 11:37

The first line of this verse reveals that the Antichrist shows no regard for the *"gods of his fathers."* If the Antichrist is indeed Arab, as we are proposing, then his forefathers (the pre-Islamic pagan Arabs, as referenced in chapter four) actually worshipped three hundred and sixty individual deities. Again, it was not until the seventh century A.D. that Muhammed would challenge the paganism of his forefathers and introduce the worship of his singular god (Allah), in the form of Islam. Thus, neither Muhammed nor his descendant, the Antichrist, will have acknowledged, or shown *"regard,"* for the gods of their forefathers.

Secondly, we note that the Antichrist shows no regard for the *"desire of women."* But what could this mean? In the past, it has been proposed that this statement may imply an asexual or, perhaps, even a homosexual bent, on the part of the Antichrist. While anything is possible, the Islamic paradigm provides a much more plausible explanation:

Islam, at its core, is extremely oppressive toward women and shows less regard for their needs, or *desires*, than any other world religion. Under extreme Islam, there are severe restrictions imposed on dress and legal rights—including the right of a woman to leave her home without a husband or male relative. In some cases, the laws are less strictly enforced, but the general spirit of Islam is nevertheless very unsympathetic with respect to women. In light of this, it makes perfect sense that the Antichrist, being a devout Muslim, would show little regard for women or their desires.

The middle part of the verse states that neither does he *"regard any god."* The Islamic creed, or Shahada, is universally known throughout the Muslim world and is commonly stated as follows: "There is no god but Allah and Muhammed is his prophet." This statement leaves no room for equivocation; Muslims are adamant that there is *"no god but Allah."* For this reason, any god other than Allah would not be regarded as a *"god"* at all.

Lastly, we see that the Antichrist will *"magnify himself above all."* This parallels the behavior exhibited by previous Islamic leaders, including Muhammed and his successors, the Caliphs. Their authority was absolute and unquestionable.

Viewed within the framework of Islam, every aspect of this verse now makes perfect sense and is easily understood. Yet, if one removes Islam from the equation, the passage tends to revert back to a mystifying puzzle.

A God of War

> But in his place <u>shall he honor the god of fortresses</u>; and a god whom his fathers knew not <u>shall he honor with gold, and silver, and with precious stones, and pleasant things</u>.
> —Daniel 11:38

Here, we learn that the Antichrist will honor a *"god of fortresses,"* or a god of war. He will also honor this god, *"whom his fathers knew not,"* with all manner of material wealth.

As we study the first line of this verse, we are reminded that within the pages of the Koran scholars have noted at least one hundred and nine exhortations to use violence in order to spread Islam.

It is, accordingly, considered mandatory for all true Muslims to fight for the cause of Allah. At present, there is no remaining religion in the world—other than Islam—that emphasizes violence as a way to advance its cause. Therefore, Allah would certainly qualify as a *"god of fortresses."*

In the second part of the same verse, we observe that the Antichrist honors his god with *"gold and silver"* and other *"pleasant things."* As is detailed in the Koran, Islam requires Muslims to use their wealth to honor, and to fight for, the cause of Allah: *"The true believers are those that have faith in Allah and His apostle, and never doubt; and who fight with their wealth and with their persons in the cause of Allah. Such are those whose faith is true" (Surah 49:15).*

Again, both of the principles highlighted in this verse fall in line with the model of Islamic behavior that was established by Muhammed. Without the insight gained by looking to the religion of Islam as the antichrist power, this verse, once again, becomes difficult to decipher.

A Foreign God

And he shall deal with the strongest fortresses by the help of a <u>foreign god</u>: whosoever acknowledgeth him he will <u>increase with glory</u>; and he shall cause them to rule over many, and shall divide the land for a price.

—Daniel 11:39

Here, the term *"foreign god"* refers to Allah, as he is certainly a *false* or *"foreign"* god.

In the third line of the verse we learn that the Antichrist will *"increase with glory"* all those who recognize Allah as god and Islam as the true religion.

As leader of the Muslim world, the Antichrist then delegates authority to those who acknowledge his rule—dividing amongst them the lands that he captures.

These actions fit the profile of one who is emulating the prophet

Muhammed or, perhaps, the Islamic Caliphs, as they swept across the Middle East—conquering the lands and sharing the spoils of war.

Once more, we find a verse describing actions that are consistent with Islamic doctrines and traditions. As we progress, it is becoming increasingly apparent that the Antichrist is modeling his behavior after the example set by Islam's archetype of the perfect human being, Muhammed. As noted in earlier chapters, a dedicated Muslim—as the Antichrist most definitely will be—is taught to model his actions on the life and teachings of Muhammed in all ways.

Beheading

And I saw thrones, and they sat upon them, and judgment was given unto them: and <u>I saw the souls of them that were beheaded for the witness of Jesus, and for the word of God,</u> and which had not worshipped the beast, neither his image, neither had received his mark upon their foreheads, or in their hands; and they lived and reigned with Christ a thousand years.

—Revelation 20:4

In this verse, John describes a vision in which he sees *"the souls of them that were beheaded for the witness of Jesus, and for the word of God."* These *"souls"* are, in fact, the people who have been *"beheaded"* for the very reason of their bearing witness to a belief in Jesus Christ, as well as their refusal to worship the Beast.

As we study this passage, the question that comes immediately to mind is, why did God choose to specify that these souls had been *"beheaded?"* During the first century A.D., when the Book of Revelation was written, the most common method of killing was crucifixion; stoning, burning, and strangulation were also used. This being the case, God could have just as easily inspired John to use more general terms, perhaps conveying that these souls were simply *"killed"* or *"martyred"* for their beliefs.

The only reasonable explanation for the mention of beheading in this verse is that it is a direct reference to Islam. This notion is reinforced by the fact that there has never been a world religion other than Islam that has practiced beheading specifically as a means to eliminate those who profess belief in *"Jesus"* or the *"Word of God."*

What is more, the practice of beheading is considered to be part of the very *heritage* of Islam. It is not only commanded as a specific method of killing one's enemies in the Koran (*"When ye encounter the infidels, strike off their heads"*—Surah 47:4) but was the favored method of killing by Muhammed and his followers.

To help Illustrate the point, we cite an example from the Islamic Hadith, which details the infamous massacre of the Medinian Jewish tribe known as the Banu Qurayza:

The Qurayza had rejected Muhammed's claims of prophethood, thereby calling into question his authority over Medina. Tensions mounted between the two communities, and the Qurayza soon found themselves embroiled in battle with Muhammed and his men. At some point, Isolated and besieged, the Qurayza were left with no other option but to surrender to Muhammed—thus, falling subject to Muslim justice. On Muhammed's order, some six hundred to nine hundred Jews from the Qurayza were led to the Market of Medina. Trenches were dug and all of the men were beheaded. Their decapitated corpses were buried in the trenches while Muhammad stood in attendance.

While examples such as the massacre of the Banu Qurayza are shocking from any perspective, we in the West have previously taken comfort in the fact that this type of barbarism had long been abandoned.

Indeed, before 9/11 and the upsurge in Islamic terrorism, beheading was considered by most to be an ancient form of execution, no longer practiced, except, perhaps, in some isolated third-world regions or strict Muslim societies. For one to suggest that beheading might be the preferred technique of some future tyrant would seem doubly odd, especially in light of the numerous high-tech methods of killing that are available today. Nevertheless, this ancient practice appears to be making a comeback.

Written nearly two thousand years ago, this Bible verse now takes on a completely contemporary feel, as beheadings have become almost commonplace in the news. Incredibly, we have actually witnessed the beheadings of westerners at the hands of Muslim extremists, videotaped and posted on the internet for all to see.

Only Those Bearing the Mark Can Buy or Sell

And that <u>no man might buy or sell, save he that had the mark, or the name of the beast,</u> or the number of his name.

—Revelation 13:17

Here, we find that the Antichrist has put forth an edict declaring that unless one has taken "*the mark, or the name of the beast,*" they cannot "*buy or sell.*" The meaning of this mark will be explored in a later chapter. For now, it will suffice to say that it is simply a way of identifying oneself as a Muslim.

In reading this verse, we are first struck by the fact that a form of selective discrimination against non-Muslims has been implemented. This echoes the long-held Islamic tradition of dhimmitude. Again, under a system of dhimmitude, policies are put in place which favor Muslims and subjugate all non-Muslims within the society.

But how, one might ask, could a singular ruler such as the Antichrist wield such power over so many? Recent developments in financial quarters may offer some clues:

Currently being characterized by commentators as a "new phenomenon" in banking, Islamic, or "Sharia compliant," financial services are rapidly expanding in popularity. In a February 2008 article posted at "FrontPage" Magazine Jonathan Schanzer writes:

"While Americans are selling their positions in U.S. companies, Middle Easterners flush with petrodollars are agg-

ressively gobbling up these stocks at fire sale prices. Moreover, as American financial institutions report the losses that forced them to deplete their cash reserves, CEOs are begging for loans from oil-rich Middle East nations that have benefited from the rise in oil prices in recent years from $30 to nearly $100 per barrel...The procurement of these loans (Wall Street calls them "cash infusions") means that our economic interests are growing increasingly beholden to countries that, at best, do not have America's best interests in mind. At worst, they are nations that could one day use their financial leverage to demand that businesses comply with Islamic law (shari'a) or even fund Islamist charities that siphon off donations to fund violence."

As far fetched as it may seem, many observers warn that as Islamic banking gains a significant foothold around the globe it becomes much easier to envision how one's ability to "*buy or sell*" might become contingent upon his compliance to Sharia.

To expand on this idea even further, some have suggested scenarios in which the Antichrist might choose to halt the sale of Middle Eastern oil to those countries that refuse to operate under the guidelines of Islam.

Nonetheless, in spite of the seemingly global implications, the actual scope of the Antichrist's order to exclude non-Muslims from commerce remains somewhat of a mystery. It is a distinct possibility that this verse may be speaking more of a *local* decree that would affect primarily those non-Muslims living within the immediate boundaries of the Antichrist's Kingdom. Such a scenario might merely involve preference being given to Muslims in regard to buying food and other necessities.

Whether this edict is more regional or global in nature will eventually become clear. For now, however, one thing is certain: This ancient Bible verse points to Islam in every sense of the word.

Killing for God

They will put you out of the synagogue; <u>in fact, a time is coming when anyone who kills you will think he is offering a service to God.</u>

—John 16:2

In this verse from the Book of John, Jesus tells His disciples that a time is coming when anyone who kills a Christian or Jew will think that he is doing a service for God.

From the disciples' perspective, it would have been difficult to make sense of Jesus' statement, as it seems to be counterintuitive. They must have asked themselves how it might be possible that someone could kill God's own people yet think that they are doing Him a service. The disciples, of course, had no idea that one day a false religion would arise, deceiving billions into worshipping a god who masquerades as the one true God. They could never have imagined a scenario in which this false god would then require—as a service to him—that Christians and Jews be destroyed.

Again, Islam is unique among religions in that its holiest writings condemn Christians and Jews, specifically, for their beliefs. No other faith fits the profile of having a god who commands the persecution of these two groups. The Muslims that kill infidels (Jews, Christians, and other nonbelievers) honestly believe that they are doing God's work.

The Breaking of Treaties

He will confirm a covenant with many for one seven. <u>In the middle of the seven he will put an end to sacrifice and offering.</u> And on a wing of the temple he will set up an abomination that causes desolation, until the end that is decreed is poured out on him.

—Daniel 9:27

There is virtually unanimous agreement among Bible scholars that this verse refers to a seven year peace treaty that will be signed between the Nation of Israel and the Antichrist. Yet, our focus here is not directed at the confirmation of the treaty but at the underlined portion of the verse, which indicates that the agreement will be *broken* by the Antichrist at mid-point, or after three and a half years.

On one hand, the breaking of this treaty is significant because most scholars believe this to be the event that will trigger the period known as the great *"tribulation"*—setting the clock ticking on the last few years of history as we know it. But the primary reason that we find the breaking of this treaty so interesting is the fact that the Antichrist's actions here parallel a well-known tradition within Islam, which is, oddly enough, the breaking of treaties.

Those who have studied Islamic history will recognize the term *al-Hudaibiyya Treaty* and its meaning to Muslims. Yasser Arafat often used the expression "Hudaibiyya" when he spoke to his people in Arabic, or when he met with the Arab National Council. Essentially, Hudaibiyya is a well-understood code word, which means, *"Kiss the hand of your enemy until you can cut it off."*

As it turns out, this is precisely what Muhammed did to the Jews of the Quraish Tribe who lived in Mecca:

In 628 A.D., Muhammad attempted to make a pilgrimage to the Kaaba in Mecca. As he neared, the Meccan troops opposed him and forbade him to proceed. Because Muhammed's men numbered only 1,400 at the time, he entered into negotiations with the Meccans and came to an agreement known as the Treaty of Hudaibiyya.

This treaty, which was to suspend war for ten years, humiliated both Muhammad and his men. Later, as he journeyed home, Muhammad told his followers that the affair at Hudaybiyya was, in fact, a "victory." As proof of the victory, he told them that they would soon share in the plunder of the Jewish settlement of Khaibar.[1]

Only eighteen months into the ten year treaty, Muhammed's

army had swelled to ten thousand men. Realizing that he had gained sufficient forces, Muhammed immediately set out to conquer Mecca and exterminate the Jewish tribe. In doing so, he established forever the obligation of every Muslim to enter into covenants with non-Muslims when necessary—this, with the understanding that these agreements would be broken as soon as it was expedient to do so.

The fact that the Antichrist will ultimately break his treaty with Israel, suggests a Muslim acting in the tradition of his prophet, Muhammed. To be sure, neither honor, nor ethics, nor obligations, can be allowed to hinder the advancement of Islam.

Changing Times and Laws

And <u>he shall speak great words against the most High, and shall wear out the saints of the most High, and think to change times and laws</u>: and they shall be given into his hand until a time and times and the dividing of time.

—Daniel 7:25

In this verse from the Book of Daniel, we find the Antichrist engaging in some characteristically brazen conduct. First and foremost, he is said to speak against the *"most High."* This, of course, refers to the God of the Bible. By simple virtue of being a devout Muslim, the Antichrist's beliefs pertaining to God fall far short of the truth that is found in Scripture. As noted earlier, the *Shahada*, "There is no god but Allah and Muhammed is his prophet," is utterly blasphemous in its denial of Christ and its claim that Muhammed was a Prophet of God. This undoubtedly qualifies as speaking *"against the most High."*

Secondly, we observe that the Antichrist *"shall wear out the saints"* (Christians) and will try to change the *"times and laws."* Without the benefit of insight, the Antichrist's actions here seem to be completely bizarre. While it is conceivable that a new ruler might desire to change existing laws, why would one attempt to change the set *"times"* or calendars?

Looking once more to Islam, a highly plausible explanation is found. In addition to the Gregorian calendar that is used in the West, there is also a Jewish, a Hindu, and a Muslim calendar, among others. Jews or Hindus, however, are not likely to impose their religious laws or calendars onto the rest of the world. A dedicated Muslim, on the other hand—having a mandate from Allah to dominate the earth—would unquestionably desire to institute the Islamic calendar on a worldwide basis if he should ever acquire the means to do so.

Once again, we find that Islam, placed in the role of Antichrist, has shed a revealing light on what has historically been considered to be a very cryptic, if not utterly confounding, Bible verse.

Conclusion

As we bring to a close this chapter, in which we have tested the theory of an Islamic Beast, it should be noted that this has by no means been an exhaustive study. A more thorough dissection of the Books of Revelation, Daniel, and many others, would no doubt yield further results.

Considering that all of the key prophetic verses we have examined reveal a pattern of behavior and attributes that are Islamic in every respect, one might safely conclude that the hypothesis holds up very well indeed. If only a few correlations could be found between Islam and the Beast of the Bible, then perhaps the phenomenon could be dismissed as coincidence.

Nonetheless, the sheer volume and specificity of these parallels seem to advance the notion of an Islamic Antichrist to a point beyond the realm of deniability. But of course, as always, the reader will have to weigh the evidence and judge for him or herself.

TWELVE

Little children, it is the last hour; and as you have heard that the Antichrist is coming, even now many antichrists have come, by which we know that it is the last hour.

—1 John 2:18

Unmasking the Mahdi

T he Bible teaches that in the end times, directly preceding the return of Jesus Christ, a great political leader will emerge. He will begin his rise to power as a dynamic, charismatic, and insightful visionary who will astound many with the cleverness of his solutions to long-standing problems. Many believe that he will appear to be the savior of the world, but as he consolidates his power, his true nature will be revealed.

The individual that we speak of is, of course, the one popularly known as "the Antichrist."

The Antichrist is, without a doubt, the most well-known of all the villainous figures that we read of in the Scriptures. In fact, virtually everyone has heard of this end-times archetype of evil, including many of those who have never opened a Bible.

Muslim End-Time Beliefs

Most people are aware that Christians hold very specific beliefs in regard to the Antichrist and the events that are prophesied to unfold in the end times. Yet, very few outside of the Muslim community realize that Islam has its own set of very specific end-times doctrines. In fact, belief in the "Last Day" is included as one of the five core tenets that all true Muslims must adhere to. It therefore goes without saying that there are no serious-minded Muslims who do not have an understanding of the events leading up to the end of the age.

Perhaps owing to current events, the central role that these beliefs play in the lives of Muslims has come under the scrutiny of more and more Christian scholars who are making efforts to understand the Muslim side of the story with respect to the end times.

Interestingly, after delving into the subject, many have been surprised to learn that Muslims are also awaiting the appearance of a dynamic and powerful leader in the last days. Though, unlike the biblical Antichrist, this Islamic leader is not portrayed as a villain. To the contrary, he is viewed as the predestined savior and champion of Islam.

Some believe him to be the *Mahdi*, or *the Guided One*, while many have a more general idea of a Caliph who will unite all Muslims as they once were during the days of the Islamic Empire. Considering what has been written about this figure in the Islamic traditions, it is quite possible that he will fulfill both of these roles.

Whichever the case may be, there is one thing of which we can be sure: The coming of this revered Muslim leader is, by far, the most anxiously anticipated event in the Islamic world. It is considered to be the central sign for Muslims that Judgment Day is near and that victory for Islam is at hand.

Curious Parallels

The fact that both Christians and Muslims are anticipating the emergence of a central figure in the end times is, perhaps, not surprising when we consider the sources that Muhammed drew upon as he formed the basis of the Islamic faith. Recalling what we learned earlier in chapter three (*The Koran*), Muhammed essentially borrowed many of the key characters, as well as fragments of biblical accounts, from the Jewish and Christian traditions.

Nevertheless, what has raised the curiosity of some prophecy scholars is the fact that while parallels do exist, they do not appear to be the result of a mere mimicking of Bible stories and characters.

Once again citing Joel Richardson's book: *Antichrist: Islam's awaited Messiah*, the author points out that numerous parallels can be drawn which highlight the fact that the Muslim end-times traditions, oddly enough, seem to resemble more of a converse, or *mirrored*, version of what the Bible portrays. For instance, the general storylines concerning the Antichrist and the Mahdi are similar, yet the role that each individual plays clearly holds a completely opposite meaning for each of the respective religions.

In the following pages, we will begin to delve into some of these intriguing parallels, as they provide a critical insight into the end-times prophecies of both Christianity and Islam. However, before we proceed with making any comparisons, it will be helpful to familiarize ourselves with each of these figures on an individual basis.

Let us begin, then, by taking a closer look at the Christian beliefs surrounding the biblical figure known as the Antichrist.

A Man of Many Titles

Surprisingly enough, the term, "Antichrist" is seldom used in the Bible. In reality, this biblical villain is more often referred to by various other titles, such as *"the man of sin," "the desolator," "Gog," "the son of destruction," "the Assyrian,"* and *"the beast."* Despite this fact, "Antichrist" has become the label most often attached to the one who will emerge under the guise of peace, only to wreak havoc in the end times. Thus, for the sake of simplicity, it is the term commonly used throughout this chapter, as well as others.

The Rise of the Antichrist

The powerful leadership role of the Antichrist is first depicted clearly in the Book of Daniel. In chapter seven, we find Daniel describing a vision of some very bizarre *"beasts."* These beasts are, of course, the same (lion, bear and leopard) creatures that we examined earlier in chapter nine. Again, they represent three, and ultimately four, very great kingdoms that would come upon the world.

After describing the first three beasts, Daniel says this of the fourth:

After that, in my vision at night I looked, and there before me was a fourth beast-terrifying and frightening and very

179

powerful. It had large iron teeth; it crushed and devoured its victims and trampled underfoot whatever was left. It was different from all the former beasts, and it had ten horns. While I was thinking about the horns, <u>there before me was another horn, a little one, which came up among them</u>; and three of the first horns were uprooted before it. <u>This horn had eyes like the eyes of a man and a mouth that spoke boastfully.</u>

—Daniel 7:7, 8

Troubled by the vision, Daniel asks the angel for an interpretation. The angel then clarifies things: "...*The fourth beast shall be a fourth kingdom on earth, Which shall be different from all other kingdoms, And shall devour the whole earth, Trample it and break it in pieces*" *(Daniel 7:23).*

Again, as we learned in chapter nine, this fourth kingdom is the one known as the "*beast*," or the "*antichrist*," kingdom. Initially, this kingdom will consist of ten kings—represented by each of the ten horns—then, another king, an eleventh, will arise and displace three of the previous kings. This eleventh king, first referred to as the little "*horn*" in this verse, is the Antichrist.

Therefore, based on Daniel's vision, we learn that the Antichrist is a future king who will gain control of a large coalition of nations—this, after seeing three of them "*uprooted*" before him. The kingdom that the Antichrist rules over will be one of immense power and ferocity. It will "*devour*" its victims and "*trample*" underfoot whatever is left.

Although this passage from Daniel does not offer much in the way of detail about the Antichrist's character—other than the fact that he speaks "*boastfully*"—it serves to give us a broader view of his ascension to power, as well as the enormity and ferocious nature of the kingdom that he will eventually preside over.

Now, in order to get a better sense of the Antichrist's personality and character, we take a closer look at some specific traits that he will possess.

Profiling the Antichrist

According to the Bible, the Antichrist will be Satan's primary human agent on earth in the last days. He will be a spiritual, political, and military leader whose power and influence will have an extraordinarily destructive impact on the Middle East and, consequently, the world at large.

The Scriptures tell us that he will be the ultimate wolf in sheep's clothing: "*...he had two horns like a lamb, and he spake as a dragon" (Revelation 13:11)*. He will initially be very effective at presenting himself as gentle, mild, and well intentioned, but on the inside he will be fully possessed by Satan.

The Book of Daniel informs us that the Antichrist is also well versed in deception. He will be a consummate actor and a practiced conspirator: "*And both of these kings' hearts shall be to do mischief, and they shall speak lies at one table; but it shall not prosper..." (Daniel 11:27)*.

Further, we are told in Thessalonians that he will be haughty and arrogant—magnifying himself in his own thinking: "*Who opposeth and exalteth himself above all that is called God..." (2 Thessalonians 2:4)*.

Ultimately, it will become clear that the main objective of the Antichrist is to displace and crush any worship that is directed toward the God of the Bible. Thus, he will be an oppressor of Christians and Jews, as they are not likely to submit to his own particular brand of worship—a worship that he will aspire to impose onto the "*whole world*."

Having become acquainted with the Antichrist, we now consider the profile of the primary Islamic end-times figure.

Profiling the Mahdi

Since ancient times, the Shiite sect of Islam has believed that the twelfth Imam—a direct descendent of Muhammad—would one day return. Islamic traditions tell us that in the year 941 A.D., when he was yet a child, the Imam mysteriously vanished after going into an underground passage to hide. The Shiites believe that he is still alive and will eventually return in the same body that he disappeared in.

The traditions hold that the twelfth Imam, also referred to as "the Mahdi," would not be seen again until he reappeared to preside over the earth as the final Caliph in the events leading up to Judgment Day. Indeed, as renowned Muslim scholar, Ibn Kathir, notes, the Mahdi is said to emerge toward the end of the age, at a time of great chaos and suffering: "*After the lesser signs of the Hour appear and increase, mankind will have reached a time of great suffering. Then the awaited Mahdi will appear*" (Richardson, 40).

Muslim scholars also believe that the Mahdi will be an unparalleled political and military world leader. He is said to "*fight against the forces of evil, lead a world revolution and set up a new world order based on justice, righteousness and virtue*" (56). Most importantly, according to Muslims, it is during the time of the Mahdi's rule that Islam will be victorious over all other religions.

While some Muslims believe that the Mahdi will convert the non-Muslim world to Islam in a peaceable manner, most traditions portray these mass conversions coming about as a corollary of being conquered by the Mahdi. In fact, it is said that "*Many battles will ensue between Muslims and the disbelievers during the Mahdi's reign...*" and also that "*The Mahdi will invade all the places between East and West*" (44).

Regardless of whether these conversions to Islam come about peaceably or forcefully, there is unanimous agreement among Muslims on at least one point, which is that the Mahdi is one whose influence and authority will extend over all of the earth.

Finally, the Islamic traditions provide two more crucial details regarding the Mahdi's rule—revealing the length of his reign, as well as the location of his center of operations. Significantly, it is said that he will "*direct the affairs of this (Islamic) nation for seven years,*" and that "*he will settle in Jerusalem.*"[1]

Now that we have been properly introduced to both the Antichrist and the Mahdi, let us take a look at some significant commonalities between the two.

Both the Antichrist and the Mahdi Will Blaspheme the God of the Bible and Lead Many to Deny Christ

The following excerpts from the Books of Daniel and Revelation typify the Antichrist's general attitude of disregard for the God of the Bible:

"… and shall speak marvellous things against the God of gods, and shall prosper till the indignation be accomplished"

—Daniel 11:36

"And he shall speak great words against the most High…"

—Daniel 7:25

"And there was given unto him a mouth speaking great things and blasphemies…"

—Revelation 13:5

Obviously, the Antichrist has no respect for God—but what about the Mahdi?

As is highlighted in the previous chapter, the Islamic Shahada, "There is no god but Allah and Muhammed is his prophet" represents the very core of Islamic beliefs. Again, the Mahdi, by sheer virtue of being a Muslim, lives and dies by this very creed, which is, of course, utterly blasphemous toward the God of the Bible.

Also referenced throughout this book is the fact that Muslim beliefs deny the deity of Christ. The following verse from the Koran refers to Jesus as the "*son of Marium*" (Mary) and essentially relegates Him to the position of "*only an apostle*." It thus becomes abundantly clear how the Mahdi—like the Antichrist—will speak against the God of the Bible:

> O followers of the Book! Do not exceed the limits in your religion, and do not speak (lies) against Allah, but (speak) the truth; <u>the Messiah</u>, Isa son of Marium <u>is only an apostle of Allah</u> and His Word which He communicated to Marium and a spirit from Him; believe therefore in Allah and His apostles, and say not, Three. Desist, it is better for you; <u>Allah is only one God; far be It from His Glory that He should have a son</u>, whatever is in the heavens and whatever is in the earth is His, and Allah is sufficient for a protector.
>
> —Surah 4.171

While on the subject of Jesus, it is interesting to note that although Muslims do not view Him in the same light as Christians, they do anticipate His return in the last days. Though, perhaps not surprisingly, the Muslim expectations in regard to the return of Christ differ considerably from Christian beliefs. According to Muslims, *"He will battle the Antichrist, defeat him, confess Islam, kill all pigs (Jews), break all crosses (abolish Christianity) and establish one thousand years of righteousness."*[2]

Strangely enough, it appears that Muslims have recast Jesus into the role of a radical Muslim.

The Antichrist and the Mahdi Both Have a Targeted Campaign Against Jews and Christians

Islamic traditions speak much of the Mahdi's special calling to convert Christians and Jews to Islam, yet they speak very little of conversions from other faiths. It seems as though converting Christians and Jews, specifically, will be the primary evangelistic aim of the Mahdi.

The following quote from Ayatollah Ibrahim Amini clearly articulates this vision: *"The Mahdi will offer the religion of Islam to the Jews and Christians; if they accept it they will be spared, otherwise they will be killed."*

In parallel, the Bible is very clear that the Antichrist will specifically target Jews and then Christians, for death (Richardson, 61).

The Antichrist and the Mahdi Both Initiate a Seven Year Treaty with Israel

As noted in the previous chapter, after rising to power, and as a prelude to his invasion of Israel, the Antichrist is said to initiate a peace treaty with the Jews:

He will confirm a covenant with many for one seven. In the middle of the seven he will put an end to sacrifice and offering. And on a wing of the temple he will set up an abomination that causes desolation, until the end that is decreed is poured out on him.

—Daniel 9:27

Similarly, as recorded in the Islamic Hadiths, the Mahdi is said to be the one who will initiate Islam's fourth and final treaty between "the Romans" and the Muslims:

The Prophet said: There will be four peace agreements between you and the Romans. The fourth will be mediated through a person who will be from the progeny of Hadrat Aaron (Honorable Aaron, the brother of Moses) and will be upheld for seven years. The people asked, "O Prophet Muhammad, who will be the imam (leader) of the people at that time?" The Prophet said: He will be from my progeny and will be exactly forty years of age. His face will shine like a star...[3]

185

The reference to *"the Romans"* in this passage should be interpreted as referring to Christians, or the West in general. The Islamists who beheaded Nicholas Berg addressed President Bush (in their pre-execution statement) as *"You, O dog of the Romans."*

Interestingly, this peace agreement is said to be mediated by a direct descendant of Moses' brother, Aaron. Yet, the most remarkable aspect of this treaty is, again, its time frame, which happens to be exactly the same as the Antichrist's peace treaty—*seven years* (66-67).

Five More Correlations

As detailed in both the Bible and the Islamic traditions, the following list illustrates yet more parallels between the Antichrist and the Mahdi. You will notice that some of the Antichrist's behavior that is detailed here will sound familiar, as it was referenced in the previous chapter. However, what makes these comparisons so unique and fascinating is the fact that the Islamic traditions portray the Mahdi as being involved in virtually all of the same actions that the Antichrist engages in.

Once more, it appears as if the only real difference between these two figures is the way in which each is perceived by his respective religion. Within the context of the Bible, the Antichrist fills the role of the villain, while within Islam the Mahdi is viewed as a savior.

Christian belief: The Antichrist attempts to institute new laws for the whole earth: *"...and shall wear out the saints of the most High, and think to change times and laws" (Daniel 7:25).*

Islamic belief: As the final Caliph, the Mahdi will institute Islamic law (Sharia) over all of the earth.

Christian belief: The Antichrist will attempt to change the times:

186

"...and shall wear out the saints of the most High, and think to change times and laws" (Daniel 7:25).

Islamic belief: It is certain that if the Mahdi were to establish Islam over the whole earth he would discontinue the use of Saturday and Sunday as the weekend, or days of rest, and replace them with Friday, the holy day of Islam. Also, the Mahdi would eliminate the Gregorian (Western) calendar (A.D.) and replace it with the Islamic calendar (A.H.).

Christian belief: The Antichrist will specifically use beheading as a prominent method of execution for nonbelievers: *"...and I saw the souls of them that were <u>beheaded</u> for the witness of Jesus, and for the word of God," (Revelation 20:4).*

Islamic belief: True to the heritage of Islam, beheading will be the Mahdi's preferred method of execution.

Christian belief: The Antichrist will attack to conquer and seize Jerusalem: *"I will gather all the nations to Jerusalem to fight against it; the city will be captured, the houses ransacked, and the women raped..." (Zechariah 14:2).*

Islamic belief: As detailed in the Islamic Hadiths, the Mahdi will attack to reconquer and seize Jerusalem for Islam: *"(Armies carrying) black flags will come from Khurasan (Afghanistan). No power will be able to stop them and they will finally reach Jerusalem where they will erect their flags."*[4]

Christian belief: The Antichrist will set himself up in the Jewish Temple in Jerusalem as the seat of authority: *"He will oppose and* *will exalt himself over everything that is called God or is wor-shiped, so that he sets himself up in God's temple, proclaiming himself to be God" (2 Thessalonians 2:4).*

Islamic belief: The Hadiths tell us that the Mahdi will establish the Islamic Caliphate from Jerusalem: "*...Jerusalem will be the loca-tion of the rightly guided caliphate and the center of Islamic rule, which will be headed by Imam al-Mahdi...*"[5]

One and the Same?

It is, by now, beyond evident that the Islamic traditions are speaking of the same individual that is portrayed as the Antichrist in the Bible. But how could this be? Is it possible that the Islamic prophecies are also reliable predictors of the future? This seems unlikely given the underlying satanic nature of Islam. As we know, Satan cannot be trusted as a source of divine revelation. In fact, if anything, it seems probable that the Islamic prophecies would be laden with misinformation and deception.

Nevertheless, while we may not completely trust the source or the accuracy of the Islamic prophecies, it appears that there is a plausible explanation for the traditions concerning the Mahdi.

Islam: Satan's Weapon of "Mass Deception"

Some prophecy scholars have noted that the Islamic traditions appear to have been "crafted" to make accommodations for the Bi-ble prophecies. Indeed, by acknowledging the inescapable reality that the biblical prophecies will come to pass, yet shrewdly assign-ing variant meanings to them for the Muslim audience, the Islamic end-times prophecies retain a sense of legitimacy, and assure that future events will make sense to Muslims within the context of their beliefs. In other words, it is almost as if a customized script has been written especially for Muslims in order to explain the ap-pearance of this powerful figure who will lead them in a war against Jews and Christians in the last days.

Could it be that Satan himself, who undoubtedly knows the Bible and its prophecies, has used this knowledge to concoct a plan that will deceive millions?

The Grand Illusion

In the Bible, Satan is characterized as being *"the father of lies"* *(John 8:44)*, as well as a *"master of deception"* *(Daniel 8:25)*. As we have learned, he is, of course, worthy of these titles, as he has managed to fool well over a billion people into denying Christ and worshipping Allah, the false god of Islam.

Since the time that the Bible and its prophecies were revealed, Satan has been keenly aware that in order to lead as many as possible away from God, he would have to pull off an illusion of epic proportions: He would have to somehow prepare the Muslim faithful for the appearance of his own agent of evil, the Antichrist.

To accomplish such a monumental task, it appears as though a strategy was implemented long ago. As noted earlier, the Islamic traditions teach that one day, as a prelude to the Day of Judgment, a savior will appear and lead Muslims to ultimate victory over all of the earth. Muhammed's own words form the basis of this belief: *"The world will not come to pass until a man from among my family, whose name will be my name, rules over the Arabs."*[6] This Islamic teaching has effectively recast the Antichrist into the role of a savior for Muslims. It would never occur to most Muslims that they have been deceived, as the Islamic prophecies concerning the Mahdi originate entirely from the ancient Islamic Hadiths. They have been passed down through the generations and branded into the psyche of Muslims for centuries on end, thus masking the true identity of this Islamic savior. As a result, millions of Muslims have been primed to willingly accept Satan's pawn (the Antichrist) as their *messiah* figure and will unwittingly follow him into battle against the true God of the Bible.

Tragically, it appears as though most Muslims will be completely blinded to the evil that engulfs them in those days. Their rejection of the truth will serve to doom them to certain destruction.

The following verse speaks of the "*strong delusion*" that will come upon those who are deceived by the Antichrist:

> Even him, whose coming is after the working of Satan with all power and signs and lying wonders, And with all deceivableness of unrighteousness in them that perish; because <u>they received not the love of the truth, that they might be saved. And for this cause God shall send them strong delusion, that they should believe a lie</u>: That they all might be damned who believed not the truth, but had pleasure in unrighteousness.
>
> —2 Thessalonians 2:9-12

The Mahdi: Coming Soon?

As we wrap up our study of the Islamic Mahdi and his alter-ego, the Antichrist—or vice versa—we turn from the ancient Bible prophecies and Hadiths toward the present day—this, in an effort to reconcile the age-old predictions concerning these two figures with the reality of the twenty first century world.

As one might expect, we find that many Christians believe the appearance of the Antichrist is imminent—but what about Muslims? We know for certain that the return of the Mahdi is highly anticipated, but do they expect him any time soon?

The Word on the Street

As it turns out, the expectation of the Mahdi's return is most definitely not an obscure or ancient belief but rather a widely recognized phenomenon within today's Islamic world. This is underscored by the virtual deluge of propaganda, speeches, articles, books, and internet blogs that proclaim his impending arrival. From the president of Iran, to prominent religious leaders, to the common Muslim on the street, Muslims everywhere are convinced that the appearance of the Mahdi is fast-approaching.

Emphasizing the heightened sense of anticipation in the Muslim world, we note the following article in which Iranian President, Mahmoud Ahmadinejad's preoccupation with the return of the Mahdi is evident. Ahmadinejad has made headlines in recent years for a multitude of reasons, primarily related to Iran's nuclear ambitions but also for infamously questioning whether the Holocaust actually happened—and for demanding that Israel be "*wiped from the face of the earth*." Yet, what has often gone unreported is the fact that he frequently references the soon-coming Mahdi in his speeches. These statements have, however, raised the eyebrows of observers who understand the significance of the Mahdi's return within the Islamic world. In fact, among these observers, many speculate that Ahmadinejad is deliberately seeking to instigate a period of global chaos, which Muslims believe is a necessary precursor to the triumphant return of the Mahdi.

Iran leader's messianic end-times mission
Ahmadinejad raises concerns with mystical visions
(adapted from Joseph Farah's G2 Bulletin)
WorldNetDaily Exclusive 1/6/2006

In a videotaped meeting with Ayatollah Javadi-Amoli in Tehran, Ahmadinejad discussed candidly a strange, paranormal experience he had while addressing the United Nations in New York last September. He recounts how he found himself bathed in light throughout the speech. But this wasn't the light directed at the podium by the U.N. and television cameras. It was, he said, a light from heaven. According to a transcript of his comments, obtained and translated by Joseph Farah's G2 Bulletin, Ahmadinejad wasn't the only one who noticed the unearthly light. One of his aides brought it to his attention. The Iranian president recalled being told about it by one of his delegation: "When you began with the words 'in the name of Allah,' I saw a light coming, surrounding you and protecting you to the end."

Ahmadinejad agreed that he sensed the same thing. "On the last day when I was speaking, one of our group told me that when I started to say 'Bismillah Muhammad,' he saw a green light come from around me, and I was placed inside this aura," he says. "I felt it myself. I felt that the atmosphere suddenly changed, and for those 27 or 28 minutes, all the leaders of the world did not blink. When I say they didn't move an eyelid, I'm not exaggerating. They were looking as if a hand was holding them there, and had just opened their eyes—Alhamdulillah!"

Ahmadinejad's "vision" at the U.N. is strangely reminiscent and alarmingly similar to statements he has made about his personal role in ushering in the return of the Shiite Muslim messiah. He sees his main mission, as he recounted in a Nov. 16 speech in Tehran, as to "pave the path for the glorious reappearance of Imam Mahdi, may Allah hasten his reappearance."

According to Shiites, the 12th imam disappeared as a child in the year 941. *When he returns, they believe, he will reign on earth for seven years, before bringing about a final judgment and the end of the world.* Ahmadinejad is urging Iranians to prepare for the coming of the Mahdi by turning the country into a mighty and advanced Islamic society and by avoiding the corruption and excesses of the West.

All Iran is buzzing about the Mahdi, the 12th imam and the role Iran and Ahmadinejad are playing in his anticipated return. There's a new messiah hotline. There are news agencies especially devoted to the latest developments. "People are anxious to know when and how will He rise; what they must do to receive this worldwide salvation," says Ali Lari, a cleric at the Bright Future Institute in Iran's religious center of Qom. "The timing is not clear, but the conditions are more specific," he adds. "There is a saying: 'When the students are ready, the teacher will come.'"

For his part, Ahmadinejad is living up to at least part of his call to the faithful. According to reports, he lives so modestly that declared assets include only a 30-year-old car, an even older house and an empty bank account. *Ahmadinejad and others in Iran are deadly serious about the imminent return of the 12th imam, who will prompt a global battle between good and evil* (with striking parallels to biblical accounts of "Armageddon").

An institute set up in 2004 for the study and dissemination of information about the Mahdi now has a staff of 160 and influence in the schools and children's magazines. In Iran, theologians say end-times beliefs appeal to one-fifth of the population. And the Jamkaran mosque east of Qom, 60 miles south of Tehran, is where the link between devotees and the Mahdi is closest.

Ahmadinejad's cabinet has given $17 million to Jamkaran. Shiite writings describe events surrounding the return of the Mahdi in apocalyptic terms. In one scenario, the forces of evil would come from Syria and Iraq and clash with forces of good from Iran. The battle would commence at Kufa the Iraqi town near the holy city of Najaf. Even more controversial is Ahmadinejad's repeated invocation of Imam Mahdi, known as "the Savior of Times." According to Shiite tradition, Imam Mahdi will appear on Judgment Day to herald a truly just government.

Missed by some observers in Ahmadinejad's speech at the U.N. was his call to the *"mighty Lord"* *to hasten the emergence of "the promised one," the one who "will fill this world with justice and peace."* Who stands in the Mahdi's way?

A top priority of Ahmadinejad is "to challenge America, which is trying to impose itself as the final salvation of the human being, and insert its unjust state (in the region)," says Hamidreza Taraghi, head of the conservative Islamic Coalition Society. Taraghi says the U.S. is "trying to place itself as the new Mahdi." This may mean no peace with Iran, he adds, "unless America changes its hegemonic ... thinking, doesn't use nuclear weapons, (or) impose its will on other nations."[7]

(emphasis mine)

Clearly, Ahmadinejad is convinced that he has a personal role in ushering in the return of the Mahdi and is doing his part in preparing Iran for Judgment Day.

In light of this, should the ever-increasing buzz surrounding the return of the Mahdi be dismissed as merely the "apocalyptic ramblings" of some religious fanatics? Or is it possible that this phenomenon is leading up to something much more tangible than most of us might imagine?

Today, there is a palpable sense of anticipation among many Muslims, as they anxiously await the emergence their savior: a celebrated Muslim leader who will be recognized by Christians of discernment as the Antichrist.

Perhaps, at this point, we are merely witnessing the initial preparations, as the troops are readied for the arrival of their predestined leader: the one who will emerge into a largely unsuspecting world to spread "justice and righteousness" for Allah.

THIRTEEN

Then I heard a loud voice from the temple saying to the seven angels, "Go and pour out the bowls of the wrath of God on the earth." So the first went and poured out his bowl upon the earth, and a foul and loathsome sore came upon the men who had the mark of the beast and those who worshiped his image.

—Revelation 16:1-2

The Mark of the Beast

I n the Bible, the Book of Revelation cryptically asserts the number 666 to be *"the number of a man"* who is associated with the *"beast."* The reader is then challenged to decipher the symbolism of this number—a challenge that has inspired mystics and would-be prophets ever since.

Today, nearly two thousand years after the Book of Revelation was written, the Mark of the Beast remains an enigma to most. The long list of presumptions and theories surrounding the Mark, while solidly grounded in the popular culture and thinking of our day, fail to provide any specific or biblically sound explanation for this puzzle.

Perhaps the Mark of the Beast, like some of the other prophetic riddles, was intended to remain shrouded in mystery until the appointed time.

An Invaluable Insight

In previous chapters, it has been proposed that Islam is the key to understanding many of the prophecies concerning the end of the age. Might this also be the case regarding the Mark of the Beast? A recent discovery has led many to believe so.

In what is considered by some to be the ultimate in irony, it appears as though a man who was once a devout Muslim may have solved one of the great Bible mysteries of all time.

In this chapter, we are going to examine what is believed by many to be the first truly plausible explanation for the infamous Mark of the Beast. The source of this discovery is an ex-Muslim turned Christian who noticed something very peculiar while studying a specific passage in the Book of Revelation. Indeed, in his 2005 book entitled, *Why I left Jihad*, Walid Shoebat brings to light a simple, yet profound, observation that will forever change the way many people look at this ancient Bible mystery.

After centuries of dead-end theories and fruitless attempts at decoding the number 666, it seems that one of the missing ingredients needed to solve this age-old riddle was an individual well versed in both the Bible and the religion of Islam, and who was also looking in the right place at the right time.

Without a doubt, Walid's explanation for the Mark of the Beast approaches the topic from a completely new perspective—one previously unexplored by those who have sought to identify the true origins of the Antichrist.

But First, Some Background

Before we delve into the details of this discovery, we are first going to address some of the commonly held beliefs and perceptions surrounding the Mark and, also, explore some of the dilemmas faced by those who have previously grappled with this mystery. This will ultimately serve to enhance our appreciation of what can only now be recognized as the decidedly clear-cut meaning that is has held all along.

We begin our brief background study by asking the most fundamental question of all.

What Is the Mark?

The understanding held by most with respect to the Mark of the Beast, or "666," is that this "*mark*," or "*number*," is an identifying sign of the Antichrist and his followers. Many also believe that the Mark will somehow be tattooed *on*, or physically implanted *into*, the Antichrist's minions. Yet, beyond these basic notions, few have given the matter much thought.

For those who seek the answers, however, the Bible does provide some crucial information about this mark: First and foremost, according to Scripture, the Mark is essentially used as a means to distinguish the followers of the Beast from the followers of God. By accepting the Mark of the Beast, one displays his dedication to the Antichrist and, at the same time, his opposition to the God of the Bible.

The Scriptures also tell us that those who take the Mark will be subject to some unique benefits, as well as some extreme punishments. For instance, the Book of Revelation speaks of a time when the only ones allowed to buy or sell will be those who have taken the Mark of the Beast: *"And that no man might buy or sell, save he that had the mark..." (Revelation 13:17).* Conversely, we learn that these same people will be subject to God's divine punishment for taking the Mark: *"The same shall drink of the wine of the wrath of God..." (Revelation 14:10).*

Is the Mark a Product of Technology?

With the advent of modern technology, some students of prophecy have assumed that the Mark may somehow be related to a type of invisible bar code system or, perhaps, a microchip implant with the number 666 encoded into it. Although, these scenarios do not seem very realistic, or practical, when one considers the fact that much of the world's population—particularly many of the remote areas in the Middle East—have yet to see a credit card, or a bar code scanner, for that matter.

Still other problems crop up that seem to render the technology based scenarios implausible. To begin with, there is the obvious difficulty associated with implanting untold numbers of people with a microchip or marking them with some type of bar code.

Further, if a microchip tracking system became a reality, it is conceivable that one could approach a person who is sleeping—or in an otherwise vulnerable position—and literally force the mark upon them, thus labeling them as a follower of the Beast without the individual ever having a choice in the matter. The Bible makes it clear that those who take the Mark will be cast into Hell. Considering this, it does not stand to reason that God would allow this fate to befall those who were *forced* to take the Mark and therefore robbed of the opportunity to exercise their free will and refuse it.

"Let him that hath understanding..."

As we are beginning to see, the traditional explanations for the Mark of the Beast often lead to unsatisfactory conclusions. Adding to these difficulties, we are also faced with the all-important question of how to decode the number 666. This, of course, lies at the very heart of the issue, as this number apparently holds a critical clue with respect to the identity of the Antichrist. This is made evident in the Bible verse that initially introduces this cryptic number:

> Here is wisdom. Let him that hath understanding count the number of the beast: for it is the number of a man; and his number is Six hundred threescore and six.
>
> —Revelation 13:18

Here, we find the "*number of the beast*," as it is referred to in the Scriptures (Six hundred threescore and six). Yet, how is one to make sense of this number? We conclude from the verse that this number is, again, associated with "*a man*," but beyond that we are given no further clues.

The Trouble With 666

In our search for the relationship between this number and the Antichrist, we begin with some very old Bible scrolls that appear to record the number 616 instead of 666. There is also a record of at least one copy having the number 665. Obviously, these inconsistencies present some problems for those hoping to decode the meaning of these digits. Even if one were to eliminate the two anomalies (616 and 665) and focus on the widely accepted 666, there are multiple reasons why attempting to decode a *number* presents a problem.

For example, a popular technique that many students and scholars have employed in their efforts to decipher the meaning of 666 is the *Gematria.* The Gematria is a mystical form of numerology that assigns a numerical value to each letter of any given name. The sum totals of the letters are then added up, resulting in the number of that individual's name.

While intriguing, there are a variety of problems associated with this approach. The most obvious being that this practice has been labeled as *occultism* by many, which is strictly forbidden in the Bible. Also, one could imagine that almost any name might be manipulated in some fashion to produce the number 666. For instance, this method has been used to identify numerous public figures as the Antichrist, including our own Ronald Reagan, as well as Mikhail Gorbachev, and even Prince Charles!

An additional problem with the Gematria arises in determining which *language* should be used when assigning the numerical values. Despite the fact that the Gematria is rooted in the Hebrew alphabet, many scholars believe, for various reasons, that Greek, Latin, or even English, should be applied to solving this particular riddle. The problems only compound from there.

Faced with the increasingly daunting task of decoding this number, we pause to consider a key question: Would God tell us in this verse to *"count the number of the beast"* if it were an unsolvable puzzle with *many* possible answers? The answer is, of course, no. This verse was included in the Bible so that it could be understood by the reader. Though, again, perhaps it would not be fully understood until the appointed time.

It's Greek to Me

Having addressed the numerous difficulties associated with this ancient riddle, we return to the original source of a recent and eye-opening discovery: author and speaker, Walid Shoebat.

Evidently, while studying the aforementioned Bible passage, which reveals the *"number of the beast"* in its original language

(Greek), Walid immediately noticed a peculiarity that led him to question whether the number 666 was actually intended to be a number at all. Was it possible that this *"number"* was originally something altogether different?

What Walid had noticed, through his Arab—and formerly Muslim—eyes, was that the Greek letters used to denote the number 666 (Chi Xi Stigma), looked very much like Arabic words and Islamic symbols. In fact, they looked eerily similar to the Arabic phrase "In the name of Allah," followed by the symbol of two crossed swords![1]

Owing to his insider's perspective, Walid recognized that the crossed swords are universally used to signify *Islam*. They can be found on virtually every letterhead within the Islamic world, as well as the emblems or logos of most Islamic groups. He was also, of course, well aware that "In the name of Allah, most gracious, most merciful," is the most commonly used phrase throughout all of Islam.[2]

One can only imagine the effect that this jaw dropping revelation must have had on Walid, as he noticed the correlations between the Greek and Arabic symbols. Incredibly, the only difference between the Islamic phrase and the Greek text was that of orientation: In the Greek text, the characters appeared to be positioned sideways, or *vertically*, rather than *horizontally*. The images below help to illustrate.[3]

The image on the far left is from the Codex Vaticanus (Greek) Bible, A.D. 350, and illustrates exactly what the characters Chi Xi Stigma, or "666," look like in the *original New Testament* text. The center image is Arabic and is commonly seen throughout the Islamic world. It spells out *"In the name of Allah,"* fol-

lowed by two crossed swords (note that Arabic reads from right to left). The image on the far right is, again, taken from the Codex Vaticanus but with the symbols that resemble "in the name of Allah" *flipped*, as the Arabic would read. Note the striking similarities between the center and right side images.

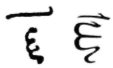

In this image, we have the Greek "Xi," exactly as it appears in the Codex Vaticanus, next to a flipped "Allah."

The similarities between the flipped Codex Vaticanus and the Arabic symbols are, quite simply, astonishing…For the sake of further comparison, let us take a look at some other examples.

Above, we have four different variations of the phrase "in the name of Allah, most gracious, most merciful," as it appears in Arabic. In spite of the diversity in style and character placement, the phrase that Walid found in the Greek text, "In the Name of Allah," or "Bism Allah" in Arabic, can be clearly picked out (toward the right side) in each version.

205

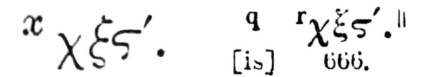

Here, we have two additional examples of Greek Bible texts. The one on the right is a Hinds & Noble interlinear version that provides the English translation directly beneath the Greek text ([is] 666). The "sideways" Allah and the crossed swords are clearly identifiable in each version.

Again, in spite of the slight style variations, there is no mistaking the uncanny likeness between the Greek and Arabic characters and symbols. Common sense would seem to dictate that the odds of this happening by sheer coincidence are beyond calculation.

Could it be that the true meaning of the Mark of the Beast has been hidden in plain sight all along?

"How has this remained undiscovered?"

Presuming that the Mark of the Beast is, in fact, "in the name of Allah," certain questions come immediately to mind; the most obvious being, how could this go undetected for nearly two thousand years? Unfortunately, we can only speculate as to the combination of events that may have led to the initial concealment of the Mark, but there is a scenario that seems plausible.

A Likely Chain of Events

As chronicled in the Book of Revelation, the Apostle John was given a vision of the future in which he was told by an angel to write down what he saw. In this vision, rather than being shown the Greek letters that represent the number 666, John may have actually been shown Arabic words and symbols that he could not understand but, nevertheless, faithfully recorded to the best of his ability.[4]

Allowing for this possibility, it seems likely that the scribes who were later commissioned to copy the original text would have been unable to recognize the foreign (Arabic) words and symbols as recorded by John. Faced with these odd-looking characters, they might have done exactly what many people in their position would do, which is to assume a mistake or, perhaps, some poor penmanship on John's part. Thus, in an effort to make sense of these markings, they may have chosen to slightly modify them into the Greek characters that they most closely resembled.[5]

While all of this is purely conjecture, it most definitely merits careful consideration and also begs a further question: Is it possible that God, in His all-knowing wisdom, allowed this to happen, realizing that the meaning behind these symbols would remain undetected until the end times? When one considers the manner in which prophecy has been revealed in the past, this possibility makes sense on many levels.

"Why is this being revealed now?"

It has been said that when God wants to bring understanding to the forefront, He enables ordinary men and women to discover what has been hidden. Throughout the ages, we find this process at work. As the time of fulfillment nears, elements of the Bible prophecies are understood. For instance, when it came time to discern the timing of Christ's birth, the wise men from the East determined from the Scriptures that the moment had come (Matthew 2:2).

Could it be that the current generation has been called to understand the prophecies concerning the Beast and its Mark, as this same generation will witness their fulfillment? While it is not inconceivable that someone might have discovered the correlations between these symbols and characters at some point earlier in history, it would most likely have escaped detection without the necessary insight of looking to *Islam* and *Allah* as being the force behind the final Antichrist Kingdom.

Again, perhaps as intended, it has not been until recent years that certain persons of discernment have cast their eyes toward Islam and its possible role in the end times.

More Translational Issues?

In light of our new found perspective on the Mark of the Beast, we now reconsider the Bible verse that initially introduced the Mark (Revelation 13:18).

In order to put Walid's discovery to the test, we will replace *"Six hundred threescore and six"* with *"in the name of Allah"*— noting what effect this substitution has on our overall understanding of the verse:

> Here is wisdom. Let him that hath understanding count the number of the beast: for it is the number of a man; and his number "is in the name of Allah."
>
> —Revelation 13:18 *(modified)*

Admittedly, after inserting "in the name of Allah," the words *"count"* and *"number"* seem to be slightly out of tune with the rest of the verse. Clearly, these words were intended to reference a *number* and not a *name*. Even so, is this awkward wording enough to invalidate the theory?

Our experience up until now tells us that minor translational issues can, indeed, play a part in our overall understanding of a verse. Therefore, focusing on the two words in question, we once again turn to the original Greek text of the Bible:

The first word, *"number,"* is translated from the Greek word, *arithmos. Arithmos* may also be accurately translated as *multitude* (peoples and nations). The second word, *"count,"* which originates from the Greek, *psephizo,* is also often translated as *reckon,* or *decide.*[6]

Obviously, when this verse was originally translated it was done so with the understanding that the original author, John, had written a number (Chi Xi Stigma) rather than a name (Arabic characters). It would then stand to reason that the translators, when choosing an equivalent for the Greek word, *arithmos*, would have chosen "*number*," in lieu of *multitude*. From their perspective, the context of the verse would seem to validate this choice.

Likewise, the same reasoning would have been applied when translating the Greek word, *psephizo*. The translators would have logically chosen "*count*," instead of its alternate translation, *decide*, or *reckon*, as it would seem to fit more with the reference to a *number* (Chi Xi Stigma).[7]

In order to illustrate to what extent these translational issues can color the subtleties of a passage, we will insert the alternate translations of the original Greek words, *arithmos* and *psephizo*, into Revelation 13:18, and then compare the modified verse to the original.

Below, we have two versions of verse 18. The first appears exactly as it is found in the King James Version of the Bible:

> Here is wisdom. Let him that hath understanding count the number of the beast: for it is the number of a man; and his number is Six hundred threescore and six.
> —Revelation 13:18

Here, in the second version, we have replaced the words in question with their alternate translations:

> Here is wisdom. Let him that hath understanding <u>decide</u> the <u>multitude</u> of the beast: for it is the <u>multitude</u> of a man; and his multitude is <u>"in the name of Allah."</u>
> —Revelation 13:18 *(alternate translation)*

By simply replacing the key words with their equally accurate and, perhaps, more appropriate translations, the verse is transformed. The references to "*the multitude of the beast*" *and* "*the multitude of a man*" clearly refer to the legions of Muslims who worship the "*beast*" (Islam), as well as the religion that was founded not by God but by a "*man*" (Muhammed). The last line of the verse indicates that "*his multitude is in the name of Allah*," further describing the vast numbers of Muslims that worship Allah as god.

Remarkably, these seemingly inconsequential judgment calls on the part of translators appear to be the very factor that has enabled the Mark of the Beast to remain an enigma for nearly two thousand years.

At this point, although we have dispelled much of the mystery surrounding the Mark by unraveling its true meaning, there is still a key piece of this puzzle that remains unsolved—which prompts an all-important question.

How Might the Mark Be Manifested?

The Bible tells us that the Antichrist will require "*all*" people to "*receive*" the Mark. Assuming the Mark to be "in the name of Allah," what might this indicate? In our search for an answer to this question, Revelation 13:16 is a good place to begin:

> And he causeth all, both small and great, rich and poor, free and bond, to receive a mark in their <u>right hand, or in their foreheads</u>:
>
> —Revelation 13:16

This verse tells us that all must receive the Mark "*in their right Hand*" or "*in their forehead.*" Does this mean that "in the name of Allah" will be literally stamped onto the forehead or right hand like a tattoo or, perhaps, encoded onto a microchip and implanted into the followers of the Beast? Again, these options remain somewhat unrealistic for the reasons that we noted earlier. In view of this, as we search for a plausible answer, we are wise to return to the most untainted source, which is the original Greek text of the Bible.

By doing some research, we find that the Greek word, *chara-*

gma, which has been translated to "*mark*" in this verse, actually refers to a badge of servitude. Strong's Hebrew Lexicon defines *charagma* as the "*badge*" of the followers of the Antichrist. Thus, the word *charagma* seems to suggest something that is worn rather than permanently tattooed, or implanted like a microchip.

Further, it is worth noting that the phrase "*right hand*" comes from the Greek, *dexios*, which may also be translated as "*the right side*" in general. This implies that the Mark, or badge, might also be displayed on the right arm and is, therefore, not necessarily limited to the right hand.[8]

Nonetheless, assuming the Mark to be some sort of badge that displays the name of Allah, what might we expect this to look like?

The Badge of Servitude

Yet once more, we note the widespread use of the Shahada within the Muslim world. As we know, the Shahada is essentially a declaration of allegiance, or servitude, to Allah and is commonly recited as follows: "There is no god but Allah, and Muhammed is his prophet." The inscription of this declaration is already worn (as a badge) by millions on the forehead or right arm. It can be seen on Muslim demonstrators and jihadists everywhere.

Note the various forms of the Islamic creed, or "Shahada," imprinted on the headbands (or foreheads) of these jihadists. In most of the images the name of Allah is easily identifiable.

Needless to say, the Bible's description of the Beast's followers receiving a "*mark*" no longer seems to be an odd concept. In fact, within the context of Islam, the idea now makes perfect sense and has taken on an altogether contemporary feel.

It is certain that as the Antichrist's Empire comes to power, and people are compelled to declare their loyalty to Allah, the Mark, or declaration of allegiance, will be worn by multitudes of faithful Muslims, as well as some who are, perhaps, merely attempting to avoid persecution—which brings up another interesting question.

Must One Display the Name of Allah to Be Considered a Follower of the Beast?

Although we have focused specifically on the actual physical *wearing* of the Mark, it is also quite likely that the Mark carries just as much meaning in the *spiritual* sense—meaning that a simple declaration of belief in Allah would *spiritually mark* one as a follower of the Beast. Therefore, in God's eyes, it would not necessarily be required for one to outwardly *wear* the Mark in order to be counted among the followers of Allah.

We find scriptural support for this concept in the Book of Revelation, which speaks of God's people being "*sealed*" *(Revelation 7:4)* with the "*Father's name written on their foreheads*" *(Revelation 14:1)*. This denotes a *spiritual seal* that identifies one as belonging to God.

It is interesting to note that the Mark of the Beast and the Seal of God are both *names* that are placed on the *foreheads* of the people who receive them. Evidently, the Beast is attempting to duplicate God's program by similarly inscribing his mark, or name, on the foreheads of his followers. This tendency to counterfeit the work of God is a recurring theme and is also a distinctive satanic trait which is grounded in the fact that Satan wishes to be like God and actually desires to accept worship in place of Him.

Conclusion

Our study of the Mark of the Beast has demonstrated that these particular verses—in order to be fully understood—had to be viewed from the proper perspective and, perhaps, from a particular juncture in time.

Once again, the religion of Islam, placed in the role of antichrist, has opened a door to understanding the ancient prophecies—exposing what was previously shrouded in mystery.

As we conclude this chapter, in which we have quite possibly uncovered a truth that has escaped the scrutiny of countless Bible scholars throughout the centuries, we learn the fate of those souls who have been deceived by Satan and have taken the Mark of the Beast:

> And the third angel followed them, saying with a loud voice, If any man worship the beast and his image, and receive his mark in his forehead, or in his hand, The same shall drink of the wine of the wrath of God, which is poured out without mixture into the cup of His indignation; and he shall be tormented with fire and brimstone in the presence of the holy angels, and in the presence of the Lamb: And the smoke of their torment ascendeth up for ever and ever: and they have no rest day nor night, who worship the beast and his image, and whosoever receiveth the mark of his name.
>
> —Revelation 14:9-11

213

PART V

The Current State of Affairs

T he attacks on 9/11 were most definitely a wake-up call for the West. Yet, remarkably, many Western leaders and citizens are still blissfully unaware of the true nature of Islam and what its ultimate goals are. While most of us are busy watching *American Idol*, fundamentalist Muslims are tirelessly plotting the destruction of the U.S. and Israel: the key obstacles that stand in the way of global Islamic domination.

In the first of our final two chapters, we are going to take stock of what is currently happening within the world of Islam and, also, the world at large. Confident in the fact that Islam is, indeed, the "beast," and equipped with the knowledge of what the Bible predicts in the last days, we can now begin to juxtapose what is foretold with what we actually see taking place around us. Do world events seem to be in line with what the Bible forecasts?

Lastly, the topic of the Beast Kingdom and the magnitude of its impact will be addressed, specifically in regard to those living in America.

FOURTEEN

Brahim: *"Nice work people; the cops are petrified of us, everything must burn, starting Monday, the operation 'Midnight Sun' starts, tell everyone else, rendezvous for Momo and Abdul in Zone 4 ... jihad Islamia Allah Akhbar."*

Samir: *"You don't really think that we're going to stop now? Are you stupid? It will continue, non-stop. We aren't going to let up. The French won't do anything and soon, we will be in the majority here."*

—Two French Muslim youths, communicating
via internet blog during the 2005 Paris riots

The Islamic Revival: What in the World is Happening?

A s the cold war between the U.S. and the Soviet Union was winding down in the 1980s, Islamic violence around the globe dramatically escalated. Terrorism, guerilla wars, civil wars, and interstate conflicts involving Muslims became common news items.

By the mid 1990s, roughly half of the ethnic conflicts in the world involved Muslims who were, in many cases, fighting other Muslims.

At the turn of the millennium, according to the International Institute of Strategic Studies, more than two-thirds of the armed global conflicts involved Muslims.

And then, finally, on September 11, 2001, the age of Islamic war came to America.[1]

In light of what we see happening in the world today, many are left wondering about the future and how the story of *Radical Islam versus the West* is going to unfold. While those who hold to the notion of an Islamic Antichrist have a reasonable idea of how things might transpire, many are not convinced that Islam poses a serious threat to Western civilization. These same people are likely to tell you that the "hysteria" in regard to the recent rise in global terrorism is simply the result of "fear mongering" on the part of "right wing conservatives and extremists."

Among those who do acknowledge the threat of fundamental Islam, there is a group who believes that the problem can be traced directly back to a poorly executed U.S. foreign policy. Many who embrace this view are convinced that terrorism will eventually subside, but only after the U.S. withdraws from Iraq and comes to the realization that it should abstain from involvement in the affairs of other nations—particularly in the Middle East.

Regardless of the position one takes on the war in Iraq, the current reality is indisputable: Now that Saddam Hussein's regime has been toppled, a new struggle for power has begun, and by all indications, the Islamists involved in this "jihad" have plans for the region that do not coincide with those of the West.

This is clearly illustrated in some excerpts from a letter penned by al-Qaeda's principal ideologue and chief strategic thinker, Ayman al-Zawahiri. Evidently, al-Zawahiri has a three-step plan for Iraq and the surrounding nations:

"The first stage: Expel the Americans from Iraq."

"The second stage: Establish an Islamic authority or amirate, then develop it and support it until it achieves the level of a caliphate - over as much territory as you can to spread its power in Iraq, i.e., in Sunni areas, is in order to fill the void stemming from the departure of the Americans..."

"The third stage: Extend the jihad wave to the secular countries neighboring Iraq...It may coincide with what came before...the clash with Israel..."[2]

Knowing what al-Qaeda's (and Islam's) ultimate objectives are, it is not surprising that Al-Zawahiri's vision includes the establishment of Iraq as a base of operations. Without a doubt, Iraq would serve as the ideal launching pad from which to stage attacks on neighboring countries—primarily Israel.

However, al-Qaeda and al-Zawahiri are not the only source of destabilization in Iraq. In fact, the pentagon has said that the *"most dangerous accelerant of potentially self-sustaining sectarian violence"* is an armed militia that calls itself the "Mahdi Army."[3]

Organized by radical cleric, Moqtada al-Sadr, in the summer of 2003, this militia views itself as the vanguard of the soon-coming Mahdi.

With recruitment offices located near mosques, al-Sadr has found no shortage of young men who are willing to *"defend their Shiite faith and their country."* Indeed, becoming a member of the Mahdi Army has proven to be an attractive option for young and desperate Shiites in Iraq's urban slums, many of whom initially welcomed Saddam Hussein's ousting but have since become disaffected with conditions in Iraq.[4]

Thus, with a flood of willing recruits, as well as funding and training from Iran, the Mahdi Army's membership grew from just a few thousand in 2003, to some sixty thousand by December of 2006.[5]

While most news agencies tend to dismiss militias like the Mahdi Army as *"apocalyptic cults,"* many observers note that Mahdist movements in the region have become almost mainstream.

Timothy R. Furnish, a Ph.D. in Islamic History and former U.S. Army Arabic interrogator, warns that we may just be seeing the tip of the iceberg: *"The Mahdi Army may just be a taste of what's to come, as conditions are ripe for Iraq to spawn a wave of messiah movements across the Islamic world."*[6]

The Future of Terror: From Bad to Worse?

Despite the obvious intentions of the various Islamic groups and militias in Iraq, many hold out hope that the so-called "radical Islamists" will eventually tire of waging jihad and settle into a more peaceful posture—perhaps opting for more constructive outlets for their hatred of the U.S. and its allies.

The problem with this view, as comforting as it may be, is that the current trends point to an entirely different scenario. In reality, most analysts who study Islam forecast an ever-expanding global role for the religion and, in turn, its radical adherents.

In view of these rather ominous predictions, our goal for this chapter is not only to understand what is happening within the world of Islam today but to identify the driving forces that are behind it. Therefore, we are going to devote the first part of our study to taking a look at what the current *trends* are within Islam. The latter part of the chapter will then be spent examining the various factors that are actually *fueling* the resurgence of Islamic extremism.

Having mapped out our strategy, we begin our look at today's Islam by acknowledging a fundamental principle as it relates to worldly influence.

There is Power in Numbers

Population Trends:

There are presently an estimated 1.2 to 1.6 billion Muslims living in the world. To put these figures into perspective, twenty-two percent of the earth's population, or one-fifth of the people living today, identify themselves as Muslim.

Islam is the world's second largest religion next to Christianity, which claims thirty-three percent of the world's inhabitants. Experts say that the Muslim population is growing worldwide at the rate of roughly 2.9 percent per year. This is faster than the total world population, which increases approximately 2.3 percent annually.[7]

Birth Rates:

Findings from the Population Research Institute (PRI) indicate that virtually every Western or *Westernized* nation on the planet is experiencing a dramatic decrease in birth rates—noting that they have fallen below the 2.1 child-per-woman replacement level. The reality is that many segments of the world's population are simply opting not to have children.[8] In contrast, Muslims currently maintain high birth rates—second only to sub-Saharan Africa.

Demographics:

In addition to high birth rates, there is another important factor to consider: In the West, populations are generally top heavy—meaning that the ratio of youth to elderly is low. However, the Muslim demographics show an opposite trend. For instance, today, more than half of the population of Algeria (an Islamic country) is under the age of twenty.

This situation is similar in other Muslim countries. These young populations will reproduce and perpetuate the increase of Muslims on a percentage basis well into the next millennium.[9]

Islam's Growing Political Influence in Europe

For most Americans, the growing political influence of Islam is not a foremost concern, but for Europeans, Islamic influence pervades most aspects of daily life. To be sure, the fifteen million Muslims of the European Union—up to three times the number that live in the United States—are becoming a formidable political force.[10]

Two trends serve to enable the growing political power among Muslims in Europe: demographics, and opportunities for full citizenship. In the year 2000, Germany joined the ranks of France and Great Britain as countries in which citizenship is granted according to birthplace instead of ancestry. The new German citizenship laws have already added half a million voters to the ranks and have opened the road to citizenship to all other Muslims in Germany. With currently 160,000 new Muslim citizens per year, the number of voters might total three million in the next decade.[11]

Further, unlike many of their fellow Muslims in the Middle East, growing numbers of Europe's Muslims can vote in elections that have the potential to literally change the face of things. Armed with the power of the vote and quickly learning the ins and outs of lobbying, the Muslims in Europe are on their way to carrying more political weight than the typical Arab citizen on the streets of Egypt or Saudi Arabia.[12]

Growing Anti-Semitism

Another trend that has raised concern among many analysts is Europe's growing anti-Semitism. Continental Europeans tend to be much more critical of Israel and are generally more supportive of the Palestinian cause. Overall, Europeans have a difficult time understanding how a small country like Israel could have so much influence over the U.S.[13]

However, a point worth noting, and what few in the West have recognized, is that the communities in Europe that are most resentful of Israel, are *Muslim*. Indeed, although Europe's Muslims hail from different countries and display diverse religious tendencies, they all share a common bond that links them to the rest of the Muslim world: their sympathy for the Palestinians and a shared hatred for Israel. Today, the effects of this general *anti-Israel* sentiment are being played out all across Europe.[14]

For instance, France, with its booming Muslim population, has been a hotbed of Muslim unrest in recent years. In 2001 alone, there were an estimated four hundred anti-Semitic incidents documented. The perpetrators of these incidents were not right-wing extremists protecting the French race from Jewish "contamination," but have been identified as *Muslim youth* of North African origin. Such incidents tend to spike upward during times of Israeli-Palestinian trouble, providing further evidence of the Muslim role.[15]

Trouble in Paris

The 2005 Paris riots may have been a mere foreshadowing of things to come for countries, such as France, who have experienced overwhelming Muslim immigration. The rampant violence, which spread rapidly across two hundred and seventy-four towns, causing an estimated two hundred million dollars in damage, serves to underscore what type of mayhem is possible when even a minority population is bent on violence.

The riots were initially sparked by an incident in which police were purportedly chasing some Muslim youths in connection to a reported break-in. As a consequence of this perceived "harassment" on the part of the police, pre-existing tensions were ignited in one of the many exclusively Muslim neighborhoods.

With cries of "God is great!" bands of Muslim youth, armed with whatever they could get a hold of, went on a rampage, forcing police to flee. Within hours, the original cause of the incident had been forgotten, and the issue jelled around a demand by the representatives of the rioters that the French police leave the "occupied territory."

Many in the media have chosen to place the blame for the riots on France's inability to assimilate its Muslim immigrants—but the truth of the matter is that France, as well as Europe as a whole, has gone out of its way to accommodate other cultures.

In this case, the French have allowed the predominantly North African Muslim immigrants to live in their own sealed off enclaves, in effect, creating independent Muslim societies within the larger native European society. As a result, police in France have more or less labeled these areas as "no-go" zones, left to be run by the Muslims themselves.[16]

A Repeat Performance

In November of 2007, yet another round of Muslim related violence broke out in the suburbs of Paris. Reminiscent of the 2005 riots, the most recent unrest was also sparked by an incident that involved the police.

According to reports, two Muslim teenagers, while riding a mini-motorbike, crashed into a police car, killing them both. Some immigrant residents accused the police of fleeing the crash scene. Yet, to the contrary, three eyewitnesses who were interviewed on television related that the police actually stayed and tried to revive the two boys with mouth to mouth resuscitation.

Regardless of what may have actually occurred, widespread

carnage soon followed. Once again, the participants were identified as predominantly the offspring of Arab and African Muslim immigrants.

Observers who witnessed both rounds of violence in France have typically noted that there was a marked difference in the nature of the 2007 attacks—mainly in that the unrest seemed to be *more menacing* than during the early days of the 2005 riots. During the 2005 clashes, the youth seemed disorganized, and their destruction was largely caused by rock throwing and arson. The aggression was, for the most part, aimed at the closest and easiest targets, such as cars. This time, hunting shotguns, as well as gasoline bombs and rocks were turned on the police.

Patrice Ribeiro, a police officer and senior union official, was quoted as saying, *"A line was crossed last night, that is to say, they used weapons, they used weapons and fired on the police. This is real guerrilla war."*[17]

An Eerie Silence

Obviously, the majority of Muslims do not approve of the type of violence that has erupted in France and would presumably shun the tactics of those who resort to such hostile acts, thus tarnishing the reputation of Islam.

On the other hand, to take a more cynical viewpoint, is it possible that this is merely a naïve or misguided assumption on the part of many in the West? If it is not, then one is left to wonder about the conspicuous lack of Muslim outcry against violence committed in the name of Allah.

The truth is that many commentators today are very uneasy about the "deafening silence" among the so-called "peaceful" Muslim majority. It seems that there are few, if any, in the Muslim community willing to speak out. Evidently, many are afraid to raise a voice of protest against their fellow Muslims for fear of reprisal—or, as some observers have suggested, perhaps there is a certain sense of silent approval in some quarters.

A Glimpse of the Future?

As the Muslim population continues to grow, one wonders if incidents like the riots in Paris will increase throughout the European countries. Today, the Muslim birth rate in Europe is three times higher than that of non-Muslims. If current trends hold, the Muslim population will nearly double by 2015, while the non-Muslim population will shrink by 3.5 percent. In fact, an Islamified Europe is not beyond the realm of possibility—and many believe that it is a certainty.[18]

Tony Blankley, editorial page editor of The Washington Times, and author of *The West's last Chance: Will We Win the Clash of Civilizations?*" had this to say about the consequences of Europe's probable future:

> *"It bears repeating: An Islamified Europe would be as great a threat to the United Sates today as a Nazified Europe would have been in the 1940s. Even before Pearl Harbor, President Roosevelt understood that a Nazi-dominated Europe would be more than a fearsome military and industrial threat: It would be a civilization threat. Now we face another such threat in insurgent Islam."*[19]

The New Jihad

In a recent statement, Saudi Cleric, Dr. Nasser bin Suleiman Al-'Omar, very succinctly summed up the renewed sense of mission that many Muslims feel today: *"The Islamic nation now faces a great phase of Jihad, unlike anything we knew fifty years ago. Fifty years ago, Jihad was attributed only to a few individuals in Palestine, and in some other Muslims areas."*[20]

There is, indeed, something very different going on within Islam today, and even though many in the West do not realize it, this Cleric and many like him are intensely aware of it. It seems that the fervor for holy war has been reignited and is spreading rapidly around the globe—awakening the general anti-Western sentiment that is harbored among Muslim citizens and nations as never before.

In light of this reality, many are asking what has changed to make things so very different than they were fifty years ago. Certainly, the doctrine of jihad is not a new one. In fact, it has remained the same for nearly 1,400 years.

The Healing of the Beast

Most experts will tell you that the Islamic revival has actually been going on for quite some time. In tracing its origins, one might say that it began with the discovery of oil in the Middle East during the first half of the twentieth century. Since this time, Islam has been slowly and steadily healing itself of the crushing blow that it sustained with the fall of the Caliphate in 1924. This slow revitalization has gone largely unnoticed, however, until very recently.

The events of 9/11 served to awaken many in the West, who were, for the most part, oblivious to Middle East politics, as well as the religion of Islam and its goals of world domination. Likewise, 9/11 also served to awaken many Muslims, albeit in a much different way: The destruction of the twin towers in New York served to embolden and inspire those who perceive the U.S. to be the "Great Satan." These same Muslims see America as the primary obstacle that stands in the way of Islam achieving its ultimate destiny.

Moreover, the "success" of the mission on 9/11 demonstrated to the Islamic world that the West is not invincible and that, perhaps, Allah is preparing to grant final victory over the "infidels." Thus, a new found sense of exhilaration has propelled the notion of waging jihad to heights previously unimaginable—essentially shifting the efforts that had already been going on for decades into high gear.

Nevertheless, in order for a mission as epic as the "Final Jihad" to be carried out, the Islamists require a support system, which consists of certain basic necessities, including funds, communications capabilities, and manpower.

But how, one might ask, is all of this being financed, and what type of infrastructure is supplying the effort? These questions and more will be addressed in the following pages, as we begin to explore the five key factors that are facilitating the Islamic resurgence and, in turn, the holy war against the West.

Factors That Are Fueling the Islamic Revival

Oil:

A turning point in the history of the Middle East came when oil was discovered—first in Persia, in 1908, and then later in Saudi Arabia, in 1938. Discoveries soon followed in the other Persian Gulf states, including Lybia and Algeria. The Middle East, as it turned out, possessed the world's largest, easily accessible reserves of crude oil—the most important commodity in the twentieth century industrial world.[21]

Since 1973, the Arab and other Muslim-dominated oil states have received ten trillion dollars. *This is the greatest transfer of wealth in all of human history.* Many Muslims have interpreted this financial good fortune as a deliberate sign of Allah's favor. Therefore, it would seem more than fitting to most that vast sums of these oil revenues have been funneled into the effort of promoting the spread of Islam around the globe. The enormous impact of this distribution of funds will be explored in more detail later, under the heading of *Saudi Funding of Wahhabi Islam.*[22]

Immigration:

At about the same time as the oil windfall, the countries of Western Europe allowed millions of Muslim migrants to enter and settle: Pakistanis in England, Turks in Germany, Algerians in France, Moroccans in Spain, and Indonesians in Holland, among others.[23]

These immigrants were allowed to bring their wives and, of course, their children; they were given free medical care, schooling, and subsidized or free housing by the countries hosting them.

These same tens of millions of Muslim immigrants are now

aggressively pursuing demands for changes in local laws and standards, including dress, family law, and freedom of speech. While most Muslims do not agree with a governmental system that is not based strictly on "the will of Allah," they do not hesitate to exploit the very guarantees of rights and freedoms that are made available to them in Western countries.

Another noted consequence of the extensive Muslim immigration throughout Europe is the fact that these immigrants have, to some degree, made their host countries fearful—inhibiting the freedom of their governments not only in domestic but also in foreign policy. This is evidenced in the recent behavior of the French, who have been hesitant to commit a few thousand troops to Lebanon—a move which they feared might antagonize their own Muslim population.[24]

Unquestionably, immigration has proven to be a powerful tool in the fight for political change in the West—ultimately resulting in an environment that is more accommodating to Muslims.

Technology:

Recent technological advances have made it much easier to broadcast the call to Islam to nonbelievers, as well as the *full message* of Islam to believers, worldwide. In the countries that had previously lacked the wealth and technology to spread the full doctrines of Islam, Muslims were able to live as "Muslims" without necessarily being fully aware of—much less following—the true principles of their religion. Though, with all of the communication that is available today, the full, undiluted message of Allah and his prophet is continuously available to those who may have been "ignorant" or unobservant Muslims in the past.[25]

The internet has also greatly enabled the dissemination of other Islamic propaganda, including recruitment and even training materials. Who would have imagined, even a decade ago, that videos of "infidels" being beheaded would serve as a recruitment tool for those seeking other like-minded individuals to join in the jihad against the West?[26]

Clearly, the World Wide Web is being fully exploited in every sense to advance the cause of Islam. Yet, perhaps ironically, when it comes to news and other outside information, Muslims from all points around the globe willingly limit themselves to Arab-Muslim propaganda, such as the Arab news channel *al-Jazeera*. The reason being that in the eyes of many Muslims the Western media cannot be trusted to "tell the truth."

Saudi Funding of Wahhabi Islam:

Wahhabi, is an even more extreme and intolerant form of Islam. The Saudi regime, whose official constitution remains "the Koran" and whose government functions "in total adherence to the Islamic religion," pours a staggering sum of money into the effort of exporting Wahhabism into the United States and the Western hemisphere as a whole.

Reza F. Safa, author of *Inside Islam*, has estimated that the Saudis have, since 1973, spent some eighty-seven billion dollars to support the effort. Much of this eighty-seven billion has gone toward educational institutions that serve to mold the most malleable minds—those of children. Today, an estimated thirty thousand children living in America attend Saudi funded Wahhabi schools.[27]

In contrast to America's parochial schools, which have long been lauded for their higher educational standards, students at the Islamic Saudi Academy (ISA) in Northern Virginia are not required to study U.S. history or government.[28]

Among the things they do study, however, are the intricacies of Judgment Day. One event that is taught in relation to this formidable day is that Muslims will fight and kill Jews. According to Islamic teachings, the Jews will seek refuge behind trees, then, much like the trees in the forest scene from the *Wizard of Oz*, they will become animated and aggressive. They will call out to the righteous,

"Oh Muslim, Oh servant of God, here is a Jew hiding behind me. Come here and kill him."[29]

Students from Wahhabi schools are also taught that "it is preferable to shun and to dislike Christians and Jews." Further, students learn that it is okay to hurt, or to steal, as long as you do not commit these acts against a Muslim.

The Saudi-supplied textbooks at ISA and other Wahhabi schools teach that Muslims are obliged to consider all infidels the enemy. Certain enemies are not even acknowledged in geography class. In fact, Wahhabi schools in America are notorious for doctoring maps of the Middle East and then hanging them in classrooms—with Israel blotted out.[30]

Perhaps not surprisingly, outsiders are forbidden to observe Wahhabism lessons, or any other classes at ISA. Again, these appalling teachings are taking place not in Saudi Arabia or some isolated region of the Middle East but within the borders of the United States.[31]

The Wahhabi effort also reaches far beyond these specially funded schools. According to Safa, the Saudis have funded more than eighty percent of the mosques built in the U.S. within the last twenty years. They have also directed considerable outreach toward the American Black Muslim community.

In one effort to showcase the "bounties of Wahhabism" to their target audience, Saudi King Fahd pledged eight million dollars for a lavish mosque to be built in a shabby South Central L.A. neighborhood. From the Saudi viewpoint, this is viewed as an "investment in the future."

Notably, as much as ninety percent of American converts to Islam are Black. According to some estimates, if the conversion rate continues, Islam could emerge as a dominant religion among urban blacks.[32]

The Saudi export of Wahhabism, via its funding of schools, mosques, and even think tanks in America—although largely unnoticed—presents a clear and present danger to the U.S., as well as the world at large, and is a key contributing factor to the Islamic revival.

Belief in the Imminence of the End Times:

As alluded to in earlier chapters, a common error made by Western observers in considering the current resurgence of Islam is that of attempting to grasp the phenomenon in terms of how we see things in the West. Indeed, most westerners tend to underestimate, or even overlook, a fundamental element that is common to all Muslims: a belief in the end times and Judgment Day.[33]

Again, while many dismiss these "end-times" doctrines as medieval gibberish, devoid of any real significance, most experts recognize how integral these beliefs are to Muslims.

French historian, Pierre Lory, underscored their importance in a recent lecture at the University of Paris:

"Eschatology represents one of the fundamental traits of the Muslim religion. The imminence of the end of time and of the final judgment is one of the oldest and most constant Quranic themes and is found throughout the sacred text of Islam."[34]

This often ignored dimension of the Islamist phenomenon is key to understanding the current revival. It cuts across all divisions within the Muslim world, including traditional versus contemporary, as well as the divide between Shiites and Sunnis.[35]

Notably, since Iran's Islamic Revolution in 1979, end-times aspirations have been at the center of developments in the Shiite Muslim world. The universal belief in the impending final judgment helps to explain both the suicidal forms of behavior that played out during the Iran-Iraq War of the 1980s, as well as the belligerent and seemingly fearless attitude of Iranian President, Mahmoud Ahmadinejad.[36]

Nevertheless, many Western observers are inclined to believe that the extremism of these Islamists is only a *facade* and that the solution to taming this fanaticism can be found in the use of overwhelming force or, perhaps, by winning the "hearts and minds" of those who hate the West. Yet, the frightening reality is that the apocalyptic mindset of many Muslims—which includes an unflinching belief in the predestined *ultimate victory* of Islam—essentially requires Islamists to fight any battle and to pay any price, regardless of the cost—this, in order to establish Allah's kingdom on earth.

Clearly, many Muslims view the rejuvenation of Islam to be a manifest sign of the truth of the prophecies and an indicator that the final victory of Islam—as well as its proliferation throughout the world—is close at hand.

These beliefs, along with the teachings of Wahhabism, ever-increasing oil revenues, massive immigration, and enhanced communication capabilities, are the primary contributors to the growing momentum behind the Islamic revival.

Conclusion

As we conclude our review of the worldwide Islamic resurgence, it is interesting to note that many experts and commentators—who do *not* hold a biblical view of the Islamic revival—do, in fact, predict a future in which Islam and the world of "nonbelievers" ultimately converge in a clash of civilizations. It would appear that, once again, the current reality and Bible prophecy are on corresponding paths.

As for the rise of Islam in Europe, we note that as things stand today, it is already difficult for the U.S. to garner support among some of its traditional European allies—particularly with respect to dealings that involve certain Middle Eastern nations. This trend, as well as the burgeoning anti-Semitic tone in Europe, is certain to grow in proportion with the expanding Muslim population. If these trends hold, and the West is someday confronted with a largely

Islamified Europe, the outlook for the U.S. and, of course, Israel, would be dire, to say the least.

While no one can predict with pinpoint certainty when, how, or to what extent Islam will become a dominant force in the world, we can be certain of one thing: Eventually, as the Bible tells us, ten Islamic nations—known as the "*horns*" of the Beast to prophecy scholars—will combine to form a coalition in the Middle East.

Some observers have noted that all of the elements required for a Caliphate to evolve are already in place. If, at some point, unity among the Muslim factions should become a reality, the world might suddenly find itself faced with a "new Islamic Empire" that would be completely hostile toward the West. This final face-off with the "infidels" would be the realization of a dream long held by many Muslims who anticipate a future where all of humanity will be governed under Islam.

FIFTEEN

"Holy War means the conquest of all non-Muslim territories...It will...be the duty of every able bodied adult male to volunteer for this war of conquest, the final aim of which is to put Koranic Law in power from one end of the earth to the other."

—Ayatollah Khomeini

The Reach of the Beast: How Will America Be Affected?

Many students of prophecy believe that in the end times the Antichrist will dominate the entire globe. According to this popular interpretation, he will hold absolute political, economic, and military power. No nation or people on earth will escape his authority.

In support of this notion, some point to the fact that this generation is the first in which this type of domination is a possibility. Long-range weapons and the nature of a global economy have, in essence, made the world a much smaller place. It is, therefore, not difficult to imagine how certain trigger events might jolt the balances of power—destabilizing conditions to such a degree that chaos could erupt and spread across the globe. Indeed, such circumstances would provide a prime opportunity for an ambitious ruler to seize total power.

Seeming to bolster the *global* antichrist theory, many commentators, today, have framed the threat of fundamentalist Islam as one that is truly all-encompassing—noting that there is literally no part of the globe that is untouched by Islamic extremism. Thus, if one were to rely solely on a snapshot of the current reality, a reasonable assumption might be that the future Antichrist Empire will be global in nature or, at least, have global *implications*.

Underscoring the point, the following factors, which have been addressed throughout the course of this book, also seem to support the case for a worldwide Antichrist Kingdom:

- Muslim population growth is outpacing other segments of society worldwide.

- The global export of Wahabbism (extreme Islam) that is being funded by oil revenues.

- The increasing political power wielded by Muslims in Europe and the West.

- The frequently stated goal of radical Islamists and terrorist groups to destroy the U.S. and Israel, with the intent of implementing Islam as the only world religion.

- The petition for Sharia Law in the UK, Canada, and other countries with growing Muslim populations.

- The widespread calls for the restoration of the Islamic Caliphate.

- The fact that Islamic terrorist groups, such as al-Qaeda, have cells in more than forty countries.

Today, violence and acts of terrorism are committed in the name of Islam everywhere around the planet, leaving no corner of the world untouched. The following list, which is taken from a website that tracks incidents of terror around the globe, lists some of the areas that have been affected by Islamic extremism:

India, the Sudan, Algeria, Afghanistan, New York, Pakistan, Israel, Russia, Chechnya, the Philippines, Indonesia, Nigeria, England, Thailand, Spain, Egypt, Bangladesh, Saudi Arabia, Ingushetia, Dagestan, Turkey, Kabardino-Balkaria, Morocco, Yemen, Lebanon, France, Uzbekistan, Gaza, Tunisia, Kosovo, Bosnia, Mauritania, Kenya, Eritrea, Syria, Somalia, California, Argentina,

Kuwait, Virginia, Ethiopia, Iran, Jordan, United Arab Emirates, Louisiana, Texas, Tanzania, Germany, Australia, Pennsylvania, Belgium, Denmark, East Timor, Qatar, Maryland, Tajikistan, the Netherlands, Scotland, Chad, Canada, China, Nepal, the Maldives…and the list goes on.[1]

Again, in light of the seemingly global picture that these indicators paint, one is inclined to assume that the Beast Kingdom might very well rule over the entire world. But is this a realistic assumption? Should those who live in the U.S. expect to awaken one morning to find that Sharia Law has been implemented in North America, or that they have fallen under the governance of an Islamic Caliph?

As we know, with respect to foretelling the future, we have only one reliable source. So rather than speculate any further, we will look to the Scriptures to find the answers to these questions—beginning with a verse from Revelation 13:

And <u>all that dwell upon the earth</u> shall worship him, whose names are not written in the book of life of the Lamb slain from the foundation of the world.
—Revelation 13:8

As we read this verse, which refers to the worship that is garnered by the Beast during the end times, we are once more left with the impression that this empire is literally in control of the entire globe. This, of course, seems to be the most logical conclusion, as the verse plainly states that "*all*" who dwell upon the earth will worship the Beast.

However, as we have noted throughout this book, the modern translations of the Bible may, in certain cases, introduce some difficulty in conveying the message of the original text. For instance, typically the word "*earth*," as used in the English language, is understood to refer to the entire planet. Though, interestingly enough, if we look to the original Hebrew text of the Old Testament, we find that the word *eretz* is used. *Eretz* can be translated as either *earth* or *land*. Clearly, in the English speaking world, the word *land* has a much different connotation than does the word *earth*—as *land* is normally used to signify a smaller area or region. Consequently, it is a distinct possibility that the Bible is actually referring to a mere region in many of these cases, as opposed to the entire earth.

Also worth noting is the usage of the word "*all*" in some verses. The Bible frequently uses phrases such as "*all nations*" or "*all the kings of the earth*" as figurative expressions. These were obviously not intended to refer to the entire world but to an entire *region.*

In light of these two important qualifiers, it is important to bear in mind that while some Bible passages seem to suggest a global element to the reign of the Antichrist, this may not necessarily be the case.

In further support of this view we note the following verse, which is a good example of a *figurative* expression that refers to a *region* instead of the entire earth:

> And <u>all the kings of the earth</u> sought the presence of Solomon, to hear his wisdom, that God had put in his heart.
>
> —Chronicles 9:23

In this instance, one might rightfully question whether the word "*all*" is meant to be taken literally. Is it possible that every last king on the face of the earth came to Solomon—including those from the far reaches of the globe, such as the Chinese, and the Aborigines of Australia? Clearly, the answer is no.

Now, using this example from the Book of Chronicles as our standard, we once again employ the method of letting Scripture interpret Scripture by applying the same principle to the verses from Revelation. In doing so, we see that the phrases referring to the Antichrist kingdom, such as "*all that dwell upon the earth,*" do not necessarily point to every living soul, or even every nation, on the globe.

To illustrate, let us take a look at a familiar verse from Revelation 13, in which the Antichrist forces all to take "*a mark:*"

> And he causeth all, both small and great, rich and poor, free and bond, to receive a mark in their right hand, or in their foreheads:
>
> —Revelation 13:16

Using the same reasoning that we applied to the previous verse, many Bible scholars would conclude that this passage does not likely refer to every last person in the world but rather to those living under the dominion of the Antichrist. Thus, a reasonable assumption as to the scope of the Beast Kingdom is that its greatest influence will be exercised within the Middle Eastern nations that the Antichrist directly presides over.

As in the Days of Noah?

There are also other verses that seem to reinforce the idea of a *regional* Beast Kingdom. Matthew 24, for example, indicates that there are at least significant portions of the globe that are not plunged into utter violence and oppression under the Antichrist. This is evidenced in the behavior of many of those who will be living at the time of Christ's return:

> But as the days of Noah were, so also will the coming of the Son of Man be. For as in the days before the flood, they were eating and drinking, marrying and giving in marriage, until the day that Noah entered the ark, and did not know until the flood came and took them all away, so also will the coming of the Son of Man be.
>
> —Matthew 24:37-39

In this passage, Jesus describes the days of Noah as a time in which people were going about the business of living: "*eating and drinking, marrying and giving in marriage.*"

Apparently, when the great flood began, the people of the earth were taken completely by surprise—all but Noah and his family. Here, Jesus is telling His disciples that it will be virtually the same when He returns. Many will be caught completely off guard—in spite of the fact that the Antichrist will be in the fullness of his power at the time.

Although purely speculative, it would seem that if the entire planet were to fall under the immediate governance of one ruler that more people would perceive something significant—or perhaps even *apocalyptic*—might be in the offing. The general state of unpreparedness described in Matthew 24 seems to imply that this is not the case.

In any event, while many believe that the Scriptures suggest a Beast Kingdom that rules over the entire world, we have found scriptural support that seems to indicate otherwise. Still, it should be noted—for those who are breathing a sigh of relief—that a hostile government need not occupy every land in order to instigate worldwide panic, chaos, and violence.

For instance, by employing various other means, the Antichrist might easily set in motion a domino effect that could reach all corners of the world—including the nations that are far from his center of influence. The trigger points for this type of offensive might include economic or political alliances, control over oil supplies or shipping lanes, and also long-range weapons or acts of terrorism.

The Million Dollar Question

In contemplating the above possibilities, one naturally begins to wonder about the ultimate fate of the United States during the time of the Antichrist's reign. Certainly, there is some comfort to be found in the fact that the U.S. is half a world away from the epicenter of the future Beast Kingdom, but has this distance merely helped to foster a false sense of security?

What America Faces

The BBC has quoted Osama bin Laden as saying, *"God is my witness, the youth of Islam are preparing things that will fill your hearts with terror. They will target Key sectors of your economy until you stop your injustice and aggression."*[2]

Considering that bin Laden and others like him have clearly stated their intentions with respect to "the Great Satan," many believe that Islamic extremists are, indeed, attempting to engineer an economic collapse within the borders of the United States.

At present, this possibility seems more realistic than ever, as most experts would agree that America is already at risk for economic devastation—largely due to the fiscal habits of consumers, businesses, governments, and the nature of today's global economy.

According to some authorities, all that would be required to initiate the collapse of the U.S. economy would be one or maybe several carefully planned attacks that would result in a nationwide panic. One is left to speculate for him or herself as to what type of nightmare scenario might unfold if somehow portable nuclear devices were detonated in several cities, or if, perhaps, food and water supplies were contaminated.

Nevertheless, most Americans find it virtually unimaginable that the U.S. could be undermined to such a degree that it would cease to be the great superpower that it is. While it is generally accepted among most that the U.S. will be struck again by major terror attacks, few among us actually believe that even a consistent onslaught of terror could eventually lead to the weakening or downfall of the world's preeminent superpower.

Yet, in looking at things from a historical perspective, we are reminded that all throughout time the most powerful nations and empires have risen to power, only to peak and then start the gradual descent into obscurity. Is it possible that the rise of Islam could be the *x-factor* that will initiate the decline of the United States and, in turn, the allies who depend on her for support and protection?

A House Divided

In spite of what the media may have you believe, many today would argue that the American fighting spirit is still alive and well. Some would go even further in asserting that this nation has not yet begun to "take the gloves off" with regard to the fight against Islamic extremism.

Though many Americans would tend to agree with this sentiment, there are those who do not support an offensive stance against the Islamic threat. In fact, one need not watch the nightly news or track the latest polls in order to come to the realization that America is deeply divided on the issue of the current war, as well as the degree of menace that is posed by radical Islam as a whole.

But this is not the only dividing issue among Americans today. Another point of contention is the perspective with which one views the Middle East and, more specifically, Israel. For better or for worse, many in the West, including those in leadership positions, do not view the region in light of its biblical heritage and see it merely as another conflict in a long line of others that will eventually find resolution—either by diplomacy or by force. This non-biblical approach, to a very biblical part of the world, may result in some foreign policy decisions that hold dire consequences for the countries involved in implementing them.

For example, the current U.S. policy is to encourage a "two-state solution" for the Israeli-Palestinian conflict. This would entail dividing Jerusalem and establishing an official Palestinian state next door to Israel. In the Bible, God warns that He will judge those who would divide the land that He promised to Abraham and his descendants: "*...I will enter into judgment with them there On behalf of My people and My inheritance Israel, Whom they have scattered among the nations; And they have divided My land*" *(Joel 3:1-2)*.

While those who do not take the Bible seriously might laughingly dismiss this warning, history bears testimony to the fact that God is one who never fails to keep His Word.

Loss of Key Allies

In addition to the threats posed by the terrorist element, some have speculated that it would be impossible for the United States to simultaneously deal with a nuclear Iran, the ongoing War in Iraq, and a loss of cooperative ties with Turkey—all of which are realities that the U.S. faces today. The U.S.-Turkey alliance is of particular importance, as roughly seventy percent of the U.S. military's air cargo headed to Iraq is shipped through an air base in Southern Turkey.[3] If the Turkish government were to suddenly shift its foreign policy stance in relation to the U.S., it could have a devastating impact on America's ability to prosecute a war in the Middle East.

An Enemy That Hides Behind Religion

In the minds of most people, the word *evil* carries strong religious connotations. For this reason, some argue that such labels should be restricted to "religious" venues. In our ever-increasingly liberal and secular society, it seems as though many people either do not recognize that evil exists in the world or are simply not willing to confront this evil when faced with it. Though it is beginning to sound cliché, moral relativism and yes, once again, "political correctness," have, in many respects, prevented the labeling of anyone or anything—particularly Islam—as evil.

There is also a belief among many today that the U.S. is no more benevolent in its worldly intentions and motivations than those nations it has designated as enemies. According to these "enlightened" individuals, it is simply a matter of *perspective*; they believe that determining who is in the wrong in any given situation is wholly dependant upon which side of the fence one happens to be standing on.

It is this relativistic thinking that has, in many cases, prevented an all out assault on evil where it exists, which has only enabled it to grow and spread unchecked. Such has been the case with the Islamic threat that we now face.

As former British Prime Minister, Neville Chamberlain—whose infamous policy of appeasement toward Hitler failed miserably—might attest to, underestimating the intentions of your enemy is an invitation to disaster.

Conclusion

To what extent America and the West in general will suffer during the period of time known as the great *"tribulation"* is, for now, still somewhat unclear. As noted earlier, it is a distinct possibility that the Beast Kingdom will be limited to the Middle East. It is also entirely possible that it might be more global in nature than some would imagine. The Bible, being primarily Middle East focused, does not paint quite as clear a picture for those in the West as it does for the nations immediately surrounding Israel.

For the time being, as we ponder the possible future state of Islam and the scope of the Antichrist Empire, we are wise to remain cognizant of the fact that Muslim fundamentalists are convinced beyond any doubt that they are locked in a life or death struggle with forces of "evil" and "unbelief" that threaten Islam from every quarter.

It has been proven by history, time and time again, that a majority is not necessary to prevail in battle. Examples include the American Revolution and also the Russian revolution, which was started by a few thousand determined radicals in a country of one hundred and fifty million. It took only nineteen hijackers to bring air travel in America to a complete standstill on 9/11. And further, not only are radical Muslims not afraid to die for their cause, they have a sense of mission, and a promise of "paradise."

CONCLUSION

And I heard, but I understood not: then said I, O my Lord, what shall be the end of these things? And he said, Go thy way, Daniel: for the words are closed up and sealed till the time of the end. Many shall be purified, and made white, and tried; but the wicked shall do wickedly: and none of the wicked shall understand; but the wise shall understand.

—Daniel 12: 8-10

The Big Picture: From Abraham to Armageddon

Archaeology, history, Bible prophecy, and current news items; predictions that span thousands of years and stories clipped from yesterday's paper. All of these have been submitted as evidence in support of the Islamic role in the end times. Yet, does this seemingly circumstantial evidence prove the case for an Islamic Antichrist?

Since belief in the Bible and its prophecies is, of course, much more a personal concern than one to be ruled on in a court of law, we are ultimately left to our own reasoning and, perhaps, a small leap of faith in order to fully accept the ideas proposed here.

However, the leap of faith required seems to be a miniscule one when considering the virtual mountain of evidence that lies before us. In fact, if one were to cast all personal bias and preconceived notions aside, thus focusing solely on what has been presented, it would seem that the truth—if not completely obvious—is at least narrowed down to only a few possibilities.

Indeed, logic dictates that we have only three possible explanations from which to choose in accounting for the Islamic antichrist phenomenon: (1) We are merely witness to a colossal web of coincidences, (2) a coordinated conspiracy has been carried out over thousands of years in which historical events have been manipulated to correlate with Bible prophecy, or (3) we are actually living in the end times and witnessing the rise of the *"beast"* in the form of a religious and political ideology known as Islam.

251

Needless to say, most find the prospect of the only plausible explanation among the above three to be alarming, if not altogether terrifying. The fact that a time is coming when large portions of the globe will be overrun by war, famine, and pestilence—followed by the literal return of Jesus Christ—is a reality not easily reconciled with most of our daily concerns, such as jobs, relationships, gas prices, or the kids' soccer game on Wednesday night.

Nevertheless, the idea here is not to turn a blind eye toward what is happening in the world but to be conscious and informed—in this way dispelling at least some of the anxiety and "fear of the unknown" that is inevitable when faced with troubling current events and dire forecasts of the future.

These things being said, all that remains of this study is to tie up a few loose ends—this, in order to help strengthen our understanding of what has been presented, and also to assist us in rendering a sound verdict in regard to the case for an Islamic Antichrist.

And so, as we close, we will briefly review the evidence, which is listed as exhibits "A" through "F" in the following pages. As we reconsider the data, we can begin to harmonize all of the pieces of this enormously far-reaching and complex puzzle.

Lastly, we will take a few steps back from the individual pieces and take in the whole scene. In doing so, we should begin to sense elements of purpose, design, and order—the same attributes that abound in all aspects of creation.

Evidence That Points to the Islamic Role In the End-Times Events

It all began with Muhammed's terrifying encounter at the cave of Hira. It was here that a being who claimed to be "the Angel Gabriel" delivered the first "revelation." Deeply shaken by the experience, Muhammed feared that he may have been possessed by a demon. Considering the dark nature of this visitation, as well as the *antichrist* spirit of the resulting religion, it appears that Muhammed's fears may have been well founded.

Exhibit A: The Demonic Nature of Islam

According to the Bible, the "*beast*" gets his power and authority from the "*dragon*," also known as Satan. This being the case, one should expect that the end-times beast, in whatever form it might take, would display qualities that are, in essence, satanic or "anti-Christ" in character.

Islam, from its very inception to the present day, has revealed itself to be the very embodiment of the satanic nature. From the perversion and distortion of the Bible stories and figures, to the mimicking of God's manner of marking His followers with His name "*written on their foreheads*" *(Revelation 14:1)*, Islam is an obvious and purposeful attempt to counterfeit God's design.

This, of course, makes perfect sense in light of the fact that Satan's goal from the beginning has been to "*be like the Most High*" *(Isaiah 14:14)* and to set himself up to accept worship in the place of God. Under the guise of Allah, Satan has used Islam in a vain attempt to achieve this goal.

For anyone who doubts that Satan is the driving force behind Islam, the ultimate question that must be asked is *who* or *what*, then, is the motivating spirit behind this relentless campaign to murder Jews and Christians? Why is Allah so intent on wiping "from the face of the earth" the only two groups who worship the God of the Bible?

Today, Satan's familiar mission statement—which centers on Israel's annihilation—is frequently espoused not only by the terrorists but by Islamic leaders and Imams, as well as many Muslims on the street. They believe that by destroying those who worship the Judeo-Christian God, a golden age of Islamic domination will be ushered in. At such a time, Muslims declare that Allah (Satan) will be the only one to garner worship.

Exhibit B: Islam Alone Fits the Profile of the Biblical Antichrist

Numerous Bible passages describe the attributes of the Beast Kingdom and its ruler, the Antichrist. God has provided these clues so that those who search the Scriptures would recognize the Beast when it comes upon the world. Though misguided notions concerning the Antichrist have circulated for centuries, recent world events have caused a growing circle of people to awaken to the fact that Islam, alone, matches the profile of the Beast. The following list highlights some of the factors that validate this view:

- According to the descriptions given in Ezekiel 38, the Antichrist's coalition that gathers against Israel in the end times will consist *exclusively* of nations that are currently Islamic.

- Based on biblical and historical analysis, the Islamic Ottoman Empire has been identified as the sixth head of the Beast of Revelation. The Book of Revelation predicts that this head (or kingdom) would be *"wounded to death" (Revelation 13:3)*. This characterizes the fall of the Islamic Empire and the Caliphate. The Bible also tell us that this kingdom will recover, or be *"healed"* of this seemingly deadly wound. Today, we are witnessing this healing in the form of the Islamic revival and, perhaps, more specifically, the probable re-emergence of an Islamic government in Turkey—the seat of the former Ottoman Empire.

- The renewed call for an Islamic Caliphate (or coalition of Muslim nations) eerily echoes the description of the "ten horns" (or kings) that are prophesied to join together, thus forming the eighth and final head of the Beast—the Antichrist Kingdom.

- As predicted in the Islamic Hadiths, the appearance of a *messiah* figure is believed by many Muslims to be imminent. Muslims anticipate that this savior (the Mahdi) will lead Islam to victory over the whole earth by abolishing all other religions—most specifically Judaism and Christianity. Remarkably, the Islamic prophecies concerning the Mahdi appear to be a mirror image of the Bible's prophecies that reference the Antichrist. The Scriptures tell us that, like the Mahdi, a primary objective of the Antichrist will be to persecute Jews, Christians, and all those who refuse to *"worship the beast."*

- By all appearances, the two thousand year old mystery surrounding the Mark of the Beast has at last been solved. While studying the original Greek text of the New Testament, ex-Muslim, Walid Shoebat, noticed something that would likely escape the attention of one not familiar with Arabic: He realized that the Greek characters which reveal the *"number"* of the Beast (666, or Chi Xi Stigma) appear to match precisely the Arabic characters that spell out "in the name of Allah."

- Behaviors that are highly specific to Islam uncannily parallel those that the Bible attributes to the Antichrist. The following list recounts some of the Antichrist's principal actions as they are described in the Bible. Each of them appears to be a direct reference to a core Islamic belief or practice:

  - He uses beheading as a prominent method of killing.
  - He and his followers show no regard for the *"desire"* (concerns or rights) of women.
  - He requires that all people don a *"mark"* to indicate allegiance to the Beast (the wearing of the Mark, or Allah's name, is already widely practiced in the Muslim world).
  - He decrees that those who refuse the *"mark"* will not be allowed to buy or sell (this discrimination against non-Muslims echoes the Islamic tradition of dhimmitude, or the forced subjugation of other faiths).
  - He wishes to impose his own *"times"* (Muslim lunar Calendar) and laws (Sharia) onto the whole world.
  - He orders that all those who refuse to *"worship the*

beast" (Islam) should be killed.

- He worships a god of "*fortresses,*" or a god of *war* (Allah).

- He enters into and then breaks a seven year treaty that he signs with the Jews (the breaking of treaties is an Islamic tradition that began with Muhammed).

- He honors his god with all manner of material wealth (Islam requires Muslims to "*fight with their wealth and with their persons*" for the cause of Allah).

- He and his followers persecute Christians and Jews, specifically, believing that in doing so they offer a "*service to God*" (throughout the Koran and other Islamic traditions, Allah commands that Muslims subdue or destroy Jews and Christians).

Exhibit C: Bible Prophecy Accurately Foretells the Future

Time and time again, Bible prophecy has predicted the future: describing the finer details of Christ's death by crucifixion—before this type of execution existed—as well as the rise and fall of kings and kingdoms before they came to be; all of this with no less than one hundred percent accuracy.

Yet, in spite of the facts, many skeptics have tried to discredit the Bible's prophecies by claiming that some were written only after the events they describe. These arguments fall flat, however, in the face of archaeological evidence such as the Dead Sea Scrolls, which provide irrefutable evidence that the prophecies were recorded long before their fulfillment.

Moreover, the Bible teaches that God does not change (Malachi 3:6), and that He is eternal in His nature. Thus, if the precise historical fulfillment of Scripture is an indicator of God's faithfulness to His Word, one can be certain that the as of yet unfulfilled prophecies—including those concerning the end-times beast—are certain to unfold as predicted.

Exhibit D: The Signs of the End Times Are Unfolding Before Our Eyes

After studying the signs of the times that Jesus details in Matthew 24, no more than a cursory glimpse at today's headlines should be necessary in order to appreciate that we are living in the days that He spoke of. To be sure, all of the signs are present and occurring at an ever-increasing pace and intensity. These signs herald a remarkable period in human history—one that is utterly unique from any other.

Perhaps the most telling sign of all is the miracle of Israel. After nearly eighteen centuries in exile, what many had thought to be an impossibility has come to pass in our generation: The Jews have re-claimed their ancient homeland and are thriving as a nation, just as the ancient Bible prophets had predicted. Virtually all prophecy scholars today believe that the generation who witnessed the rebirth of Israel in 1948 will be alive to see the Second Coming of Christ.

Significantly, in May of 2008, Israel celebrated its sixtieth anniversary as a nation.

Exhibit E: The Global Islamic Resurgence

The thesis of this book essentially proposes two things: (1) We are currently living in the end times, and (2) Islam is the Beast that is described in the Bible. If our theory is correct, then one might expect the Beast to be awakening and likewise positioning itself to assume its role in the end-times events.

Indeed, it appears that Islam is doing just that. It is widely acknowledged that current global trends point to a dominating role for Islam in the future. Experts cite booming Muslim population growth and massive immigration throughout Europe and the West.

Due, in large part, to these two factors, the growing Muslim political power in Europe has already influenced both the domestic and foreign policies of major European countries. Many commentators ominously predict an "Islamified Europe" within a decade or two.

Further, the events of 9/11 signaled the beginning of a new era, emboldening Muslims around the globe with the perception that the U.S. is more vulnerable than some had believed. Consequently, the rallying cry for the "Final Jihad" against Europe and the West continues to gain support and has propelled the campaign for a worldwide holy war against the "infidels" to new heights.

Exhibit F: The Current Landscape of the Middle East

In addition to the global posturing of Islam, it appears that the home of the Beast (the Middle East) is also in synch with the blueprint of the end-times events as outlined in the Bible. The recent political maneuverings of key nations, such as Turkey, Syria, Iran, and Israel, among others, seem to support the notion that the culmination of the prophecies may not be far off.

The following list highlights the reality that all of the necessary pieces are in place. In fact, some prophecy experts would argue that the first "domino" may have already been toppled.

- The removal of Saddam Hussein's regime in Iraq has proven to be a major source of destabilization in the Middle East—creating a power vacuum that various Islamic factions are scrambling to fill. The fall of Iraq may prove to be a critical link in the chain of events that will lead to the formation of a new Caliphate.

- Identified as a principal player in the Antichrist's coalition, the Republic of Turkey has, in recent years, seen significant shifts in government and policy—the most obvious being the election of its first ever Islamic president. Moreover, many observers note a subtle cooling of relations with the West, as Turkey establishes closer ties with its Arab neighbors. Today, after eighty-five years of secularism, many commentators are predicting Turkey's descent into the Islamic origins of its predecessor, the Ottoman Empire.

- In early 2008, Syrian President, Bashar Assad, confirmed that Israel and Syria have been engaging in secret talks mediated by Turkey. This is significant in that based solely on Scripture many prophecy scholars believe that the *peacemaker* who will eventually be revealed as the Antichrist must emerge from either Turkey or Syria.

- Iran, also identified by Ezekiel as part of the Antichrist's coalition, refuses to back away from its nuclear ambitions. Iranian President Ahmadinejad remains defiant toward the West, as he earnestly prepares his country for the imminent return of the twelfth Imam, or *Mahdi*.

- Supported by China and Russia, Iran is currently funding, training, and equipping insurgents who are launching attacks against U.S. and coalition forces in Iraq. Most notable among these insurgents is an ever-growing Shiite militia known as the "Mahdi Army." Formed in 2003, following the collapse of Saddam Hussein's regime, the Mahdi Army has often been described by the press as a mere "militia with political aspirations," yet this group claims itself to be the armed vanguard of the coming Mahdi.

- Increasing oil demand by China and India, along with the threat of wars in the Middle East, has some analysts predicting two hundred dollar-a-barrel oil. If further violence erupts among the Arab states, the repercussions will be felt around the globe, as the cost of energy, home heating, and food prices will skyrocket to heights previously unimagined. Some prophecy experts speculate that the global economic difficulties associated with a disruption in oil and food supplies would likely spark further "resource wars" and may turn out to be a key contributing factor to the chaos, war, and famine that the Bible predicts during the days of great *"tribulation."*

On the Brink

Now more than ever, the Middle East appears to be on the brink of an all-engulfing war. The still unclear future of Iraq, as well as the possibility of a confrontation with Iran, lend to an atmosphere of uncertainty and expectation. Is it possible that this current state of tension will lead to the signing of a peace treaty between Israel and Syria? Or will things merely continue on their present course until such a time that the Arab nations come to the realization that in order to decisively defeat Israel—and ultimately the West—they must unite in their efforts?

Judging by the recent rhetoric of Islamic organizations, such as al-Qaeda, HAMAS, Hizbullah, and others, it appears as though Muslim unity is most definitely the theme of the hour. In light of this, it seems highly plausible that, at some point, a number of Islamic states might temporarily set aside their tribal differences and unite in a common cause. The forming of an Islamic Union, or Caliphate, would undoubtedly fuel the fire of the *global* Jihad—emboldening Muslims from all corners of the world to join in the final frenzied battle for Islam.

Behind the Curtain

Having sketched out what appears, at first glance, to be an utterly hopeless picture of the future, let us take a moment to reflect on what these seemingly dire circumstances actually portend.

If it were somehow possible to get a glimpse of the forces at work behind the scenes, we would at once be reminded that there is something much larger at play here than what we observe on the surface. It goes beyond the presumably political motivations and aspirations of nations and rulers. It is bigger than the "Palestinian Issue," the "contested holy sites," or even the ancient Arab-Islamic hatred that has been passed down through the centuries.

Some refer to it as "spiritual warfare" or "a battle between dark and light." Many would say that it started with Jacob and Esau;

though, it may be more accurate to say that it began in the Garden of Eden or, perhaps, with the fall of Satan. Regardless of the precise origin of this timeless struggle, it is clear that the battle we are witnessing between Islam and the world of "nonbelievers" today has its roots in the larger, yet unseen, war that Satan has been waging against mankind since the beginning of creation.

The time is now short—and Satan knows this. We can therefore rest assured that he will do everything in his power to doom as many as possible to the same destiny that lies in wait for him and the other fallen angels.

In spite of this, we take comfort in the fact that as things continue to worsen in this world, the day of salvation for believers in Christ grows nearer. Until that day arrives, we can remain confident in the fact that all of these circumstances—regardless of how hopeless they may appear to us—ultimately serve God's purpose.

Through the Lens of Prophecy

For most of us, world events such as the ongoing unrest in the Middle East or the devastating effects of Hurricane Katrina are experienced second hand—via sound bites or short blurbs on the nightly news.

To the casual observer, most of these appear to be nothing more than a series of unrelated happenings, unfolding randomly in an increasingly chaotic world. Nevertheless, as we step back to view the entire scene through the lens of Bible prophecy, these seemingly incidental happenings suddenly coalesce into a concise and very telling picture—one that mirrors the intricate web of events that are foretold in the Bible.

Earthquakes, storms, floods, wars, famine, and pestilence, as well as a proliferation of knowledge and travel, were predicted nearly two thousand years ago. All of these things are coming to pass, today, and with startling frequency—much like the "birth pains" that Jesus describes in Matthew 24.

Indeed, the signs of the times and the resurgence of Islam each play an integral role in the final chapter of an epoch story that began long ago, with Abraham.

The Big Picture: From Abraham to Armageddon

Down through the ages, the sons of Jacob have survived trials, persecution, and thousands of years in exile from their homeland. The Scriptures foretold the dispersion of the Jews and also of their regathering toward the end of the age. After a long absence from a country left in desolation, the Jews have come home to the land that God promised to Abraham: "*...a land that has recovered from war, whose people were gathered from many nations to the mountains of Israel, which had long been desolate. They had been brought out from the nations, and now all of them live in safety*" *(Ezekiel 38:8)*.

The other branch of Abraham's family—the sons of Ishmael—are the Islamic Arabs that inhabit the lands surrounding Israel. Ishmael's descendants epitomize the spirit and temperament that the Bible predicted more than three millennia ago: "*...his hand will be against everyone and everyone's hand against him, and he will live in hostility toward all his brothers*" *(Genesis 16:12)*.

The Prophet Ezekiel tells us that these same sons of Ishmael will be among the enemies who seek to destroy Israel in the end times: "*And thou shalt come up against my people of Israel, as a cloud to cover the land; it shall be in the latter days, and I will bring thee against my land...*" *(Ezekiel 38:16)*.

The day is soon coming when Ishmael's descendants will unite as one: "*...they receive authority for one hour as kings with the beast.*" Their ultimate purpose being the fulfillment of a long-held dream: the annihilation of Israel. Muslims have been taught for centuries that the Last Day will not come until they wage a final war against the Jews and rid the world of them once and for all. They believe that only after this is accomplished will Muslims enjoy a golden age of peace, justice, and worldwide Islamic rule.

However, the Bible tells us that God has other plans: Before

Israel can be destroyed He is going to intervene, and bring to ruin those who seek her destruction. On that day, multitudes of Jews will realize that Jesus is Messiah, and many Muslims will realize that they have made a fateful mistake.

Though most are unaware, we, today, are witnessing the fruition of seeds that were planted nearly four thousand years ago with the birth of Abraham's sons. God promised Abraham that He would make great nations of both Isaac and Ishmael. To be sure, one would be hard pressed to argue that He did not. The Jewish and Arabic peoples have had an immeasurable impact on the world and can now be found at center stage in the arena of world politics and conflict. Thus, the history of mankind will reach its pinnacle, essentially where it began, in a region literally located at the center of the globe; more specifically, Israel and the nations that surround her.

From our vantage point in time, it is now clear that things have come nearly full circle. It appears that the stage has been set for the final act. What lies ahead promises to be a harrowing performance for those who are not familiar with the story line. Yet, for those who understand the Bible's prophecies and who have put their faith and trust in God, there is utter assurance and peace of mind that things do end very well indeed...

And I John saw the holy city, new Jerusalem, coming down from God out of heaven, prepared as a bride adorned for her husband. And I heard a great voice out of heaven saying, Behold, the tabernacle of God is with men, and he will dwell with them, and they shall be his people, and God himself shall be with them, and be their God. And God shall wipe away all tears from their eyes; and there shall be no more death, neither sorrow, nor crying, neither shall there be any more pain: for the former things are passed away.

—Revelation 21:2-4

Selected Bibliography

Benware, Paul, *Understanding End Times Prophecy*, (Moody publishers, 1995, 2006).

Fortner, Michael, *The Scarlet Beast*, (White Stone press, Lawton, OK, 2006).

Livingston, Robert, *Christianity and Islam: The Final Clash*, (Pleasant Word, 2006).

McDowell, Josh, *Evidence for Christianity*, (Nelson Reference & Electronic, 2006).

Richardson, Joel, *Antichrist: Islam's Awaited Messiah*, (Pleasant Word, 2006).

Shoebat, Walid and Richardson, Joel, *God's war on Terror*, (Top Executive Media, 2008).

Shoebat, Walid, *Why I Left Jihad*, (Top Executive Media, 2005).

Strobel, Lee, *The Case for Christ*, (Zondervan, 1998).

Endnotes

Chapter One: Origins

1. *Arab-Israeli Conflict*,
   http://en.wikipedia.org/wiki/Arab-Israeli_conflict (accessed June 28, 2008).
2. Aaron Klein, *Terror group broadcasting from Temple Mount*, WorldNet Daily, September 18, 2007,
   http://www.worldnetdaily.com/news/article.asp?ARTICLE_ID=57699 (accessed June 28, 2008).
3. *The Sons of Abraham*,
   http://www.ucg.org/booklets/me/sonsabraham.asp (accessed June 28, 2008).
4. Ibid.
5. Ibid.
6. Ibid.

Chapter Two: Islam: A Brief History

1. *Mecca*, http://en.wikipedia.org/wiki/Mecca (accessed June 26, 2008).
2. *The Life of Muhammed: An Inconvenient Truth*,
   http://www.thereligionofpeace.com/Pages/History.htm (accessed June 26, 2008).
3. *Muhammed*,
   http://en.wikipedia.org/wiki/Muhammed#Wives_and_children (accessed June 26, 2008).
4. *The Life of Muhammed: An Inconvenient Truth*,
   http://www.thereligionofpeace.com/Pages/History.htm (accessed March 6, 2008).
5. Prophet of Doom, *With Whom Am I speaking*?
   http://www.prophetofdoom.net/Prophet_of_Doom_07_With_Whom_Am_I_Speaking.Islam (accessed June 26, 2008).
6. *Muhammed*,
   http://www.themystica.com/mystica/articles/m/muhammad.html (accessed June 26, 2008).
7. ibid.
8. ibid.
9. ibid.

10. http://www.masnet.org/news.asp?id=3814
11. Islam Watch,
    http://www.islam-watch.org/ma_khan/Raihan/Challenge2.htm (accessed
    June 26, 2008).
12. Menachem Ben Sasson, *The Jews of Medina rejected the prophecy of Muhammad*,
    http://www.myjewishlearning.com/history_community/Ancient/Intergroup
    TO/Jewsand_Arabs.htm (accessed June 26, 2008).
13. *Beginnings of armed conflict*,
    http://en.wikipedia.org/wiki/Muhammad_in_Medina#Beginnings_of_armed
    _conflict (accessed July 2, 2008).
14. *The Life of Muhammed: An Inconvenient truth*,
    http://www.thereligionofpeace.com/Pages/History.htm (accessed July 2,
    2008).
15. *Conquest of Mecca*,
    http://en.wikipedia.org/wiki/Conquest_of_Mecca (accessed July 2, 2008).
16. *The Origin of Islamic Imperialism*
    http://www.thereligionofpeace.com/Pages/History.ht (accessed July 2,
    2008).
17. *Violence*,
    http://www.thereligionofpeace.com/Quran/023-violence.htm (accessed
    July 2, 2008).
18. ibid.
19. ibid.
20. ibid.
21. David B. Kopel, *Dhimmitude and Disarmament*, George Mason University
    Civil Rights Law Journal
    http://209.85.173.104/search?q=cache:_K2_ATaNwlUJ:www. law.gmu.edu/
    gmucrlj/docs/kopel.doc+dhimmis+could+not+re (accessed July 2, 2008).
22. ibid.
23. ibid.
24. ibid.
25. *Turkey, Nature of the Decline*
    http://www.cartage.org.lb/en/themes/GeogHist/histories/history/hiscountries
    /T/turkey.html (accessed July 2, 2008).
26. Kristine Steakley, *The Horror of 1915*, Breakpoint,
    http://www.breakpoint.org/listingarticle.asp?ID=6838 (accessed July 2,
    2008).

Chapter Three: The Koran

1. Christian Apologetics & Research Ministry, *Muhammed*,
   http://www.carm.org/islam/muhammad.htm (accessed July 2, 2008).
2. Christian Apologetics & Research Ministry, *Quran*,
   http://www.carm.org/islam/koran.htm (accessed July 2, 2008).

3. Economist.Com, *The Battle of the Books*,
http://www.economist.com/world/international/displaystory.cfm?story_id=
10311317 (accessed July 2, 2008).

4. ibid.

5. Word Source, *Koran*,
http://jesus-messiah.com/html/quran.html (accessed July 2, 2008).

6. ChristianAnswers.Net, *How does the Qur'an compare to the Book of Genesis on the great events of history?*
http://www.christiananswers.net/q-aig/quran-genesis.html (accessed July 2, 2008).

7. Joel Richardson, *Antichrist: Islam's Awaited Messiah* (Enumclaw, WA: Pleasant Word, 2006). p. 34-35

8. ibid. p. 170,171

9. *Violence*,
http://www.thereligionofpeace.com/Quran/023-violence.htm (accessed July 2, 2008).

Chapter Four: Who Is Allah?

1. Kathleen parker, *Oh, Allah, Won't You Buy Me a Mercedes Benz?*
The Washington Post Writers Group,
http://www.postwritersgroup.com/archives/park070817.htm (accessed July 2, 2008).

2. WorldNetDaily, *Testing the Faith*,
http://www.worldnetdaily.com/news/article.asp?ARTICLE_ID6 =5802 (accessed July 2, 2008).

3. Allah – The Moon God, *The Archeology of The Middle East*,
http://users.hubwest.com/prophet/islam/moongod.htm (accessed July 2, 2008).

4. The Call to Prayer, *Understanding Islam's God*,
http://thecalltoprayer.com/Understanding%20Islams%20God.html (accessed July 2, 2008).

5. Muslims Internet Directory, *Asma'ul Husna: The 99 Beautiful Names of Allah*,
http://www.2muslims.com/directory/Detailed/227599.shtml (accessed July 2, 2008).

Chapter Five: Islamic Law

1. *Sharia*,
http://en.wikipedia.org/wiki/Sharia (accessed July 2, 2008).

2. Citizens Against Sharia,
http://citizensagainstsharia.wordpress.com/ (accessed July 2, 2008).

3. Religious Tolerance.org, *Punishment for Non-marital Sex in Islam*,
http://www.religioustolerance.org/isl_adul1.htm (accessed July 4, 2008).

4. ibid.
5. ibid.
6. Graeme Wilson, *Young, British Muslims 'getting more radical,'* Telegraph.co.uk, January 30, 2007, http://www.telegraph.co.uk/news/uknews/1540895/Young%2C-British-Muslims-%27getting-more-radical%27.html (accessed July 2, 2008).
7. BBC News, *Sharia law move quashed in Canada*, September 12, 2005, http://news.bbc.co.uk/2/hi/americas/4236762.stm (accessed July 2, 2008).
8. ibid.

Chapter Six: The Caliphate

1. *Caliph*, http://en.wikipedia.org/wiki/Caliph (accessed July 2, 2008).
2. Melissa Snell, *Medieval History: About Abu Bakr*, About.com, http://historymedren.about.com/od/bwho/p/who_abu_bakr.htm (accessed July 2, 2008).
3. ibid.
4. ibid.
5. *Caliphate*, http://en.wikipedia.org/wiki/Caliphate#Umayyads.2C_7th-8th_century (accessed July 2, 2008).
6. ibid.
7. Bernard Lewis, *The Revolt of Islam*, The New Yorker, November 19, 2001, http://humanities.psydeshow.org/political/lewis.htm (accessed July 2, 2008).
8. *Caliphate*, http://en.wikipedia.org/wiki/Caliphate#Islamist_call (accessed July 2, 2008).
9. Yaakov Lappin, '*Establish Islamic State,*' Ynetnews.com, August 5, 2007, http://www.ynetnews.com/articles/0,7340,L-3433932,00.html (accessed July 2, 2008).
10. Middle East Media research Institute, *excerpts from a speech by Muhammad Taher Al-rouq* http://www.memri.org/bin/articles.cgi?Page=archives&Area= sd&ID= SP1 79107 (accessed July 2, 2008).
11. Hyscience, *Global jihad group debuts in gaza*, http://www.hyscience.com/archives/2006/08/jihad_alert_the.php (accessed July 2, 2008).
12. Salim Osman, *Call to revive caliphate in Indonesia*, Straits Times, http://app.mfa.gov.sg/pr/read_content.asp?View,7929, (accessed July 2, 2008).
13. ibid.
14. Jay Tolson, *Caliph Wanted: Why An old Islamic institution resonates with many Muslims today*, USnews.com, January 2, 2008,

http://www.usnews.com/articles/news/world/2008/01/02/caliph-wanted.
html (accessed July 2, 2008).

15. Michael Scheuer, *Is Zawahiri Striving for Islamist Unity in Preparation for New Attack?* The Jamestown Foundation,
http://www.jamestown.org/terrorism/news/article.php?articleid= 2373554 (accessed July 2, 2008).

16. Right Truth, *The call for a world-wide Caliphate - it's official*,
http://righttruth.typepad.com/right_truth/2006/03/the_call_for_a_.html (accessed July 2, 2008).

17. Dr. Rachel Ehrenfeld, *The Caliphate is Coming*, FrontPageMagazine.com,
http://www.frontpagemag.com/Articles/Read.aspx?GUID=9446CA77-BD91-4D8B-8AA6-00FCC2F0F8CA (accessed July 2, 2008).

18. *Yellow Badge*,
http://en.wikipedia.org/wiki/Yellow_badge (accessed July 2, 2008).

19. David J. Jonsson, *Caliphatism - Establishing the Kingdom of Allah,* Global politician,
http://www.globalpolitician.com/23423-caliphate-islamism (accessed July 2, 2008).

20. Efraim Karsh, *Islam's Imperial Dreams*, The Wall street Journal, April 4, 2006,
http://www.opinionjournal.com/federation/feature/?id=110008181 (accessed July 2, 2008).

Chapter Seven: Bible Prophecy Fulfilled

1. James Randi educational Foundation, One Million Dollar Paranormal Challenge,
http://www.randi.org/joom/content/view/38/31 (accessed July 2, 2008).

2. The Straight Dope, *Did the U.S. government fund psychic research?*
http://www.straightdope.com/mailbag/mpsychicfed.html (accessed July 2, 2008).

3. ibid.

4. ibid.

5. Snopes.com, *False Prophecy*,
http://www.n6iap.com/WTC-attack/proficy.html (accessed July 2, 2008).

6. Scriptural Evidence that the Rapture Takes Place After the Tribulation,
http://www.logosapostolic.org/studies/RP355Rapture3.htm (accessed July 2, 2008).

7. David A. Reed, *Why Believe the Bible?*
http://www.whybelievebible.com/ (accessed July 2, 2008).

8. All About Archaeology, *Dead Sea Scrolls – A Compelling Find*,
http://www.allaboutarchaeology.org/dead-sea-scrolls.htm (accessed July 2, 2008).

9. *History of Crucifixion*,
http://en.wikipedia.org/wiki/Crucifixion#Roman_Empire

(accessed July 2, 2008).
10. All About Christ, *Jesus' Nails*,
    http://www.allaboutjesuschrist.org/jesus-nails-faq.htm
11. Lee Strobel, *The Case for Christ* (Grand Rapids Michigan: Zondervan,
    1998). p. 199
12. Cahleen Shrier, Ph.D, *The Science of Crucifixion*, Azusa Pacific
    University,
    http://www.apu.edu/infocus/2002/03/crucifixion/ (accessed July 2, 2008).
13. Josh Mcdowell, *Evidence for Christianity* (Nashville, Tennessee: Nelson
    Reference & Electronic, 2006). p. 173,174
14. ibid p. 174
15. George Konig, *Zion Would Be "Plowed Like a Field,"* AboutBibleProph-
    ecy.com,
    http://www.aboutbibleprophecy.com/micah_3_11.htm (accessed July 2,
    2008).
16. George Konig, *Exile of Israel*, AboutBibleProphecy.com,
    http://www.aboutbibleprophecy.com/exile.htm (accessed July 2, 2008).
17. Isaiah Foretold the Re-birth of Israel,
    http://www.therefinersfire.org/israel_born_in_one_day.htm (accessed July 2,
    2008).
18. FalseMessiahs.com, *Jacob's descendants would regain control of Israel*,
    http://www.falsemessiahs.com/bible_prophecy/israel/past_present_fu
    ture.htm (accessed July 2, 2008).

Chapter Eight: Signs of the Times

1. By John Zarrella and Patrick Oppmann, *Pastor with 666 tattoo claims to
   be divine*, CNN.com, February 19, 2007,
   http://www.cnn.com/2007/US/02/16/miami.preacher/ (accessed July 2,
   2008).
2. End Times Stats,
   http://www.liferesearchuniversal.com/etstats1.html (accessed July 2,
   2008).
3. ibid.
4. ibid.
5. Annie Schleicher, *World Hunger on the Rise*, PBS Newshour Extra,
   http://www.pbs.org/newshour/extra/features/july-dec04/hunger _12-08.html
   (accessed July 2, 2008).
6. American Jewish World Service, *The Food Crisis of 2008: A "Silent
   Tsunami"*
   http://www.ajws.org/who_we_are/news/archives/features/the_food_crisis_
   of_2008.html (accessed July 2, 2008).
7. Andrew Gumbel, *Haiti food riots could spread as world prices rise, IMF
   warns*, Independent, The (London), April 14, 2008,
   http://findarticles.com/p/articles/mi_qn4158/is_20080414/ai_n25163985

(accessed July 2, 2008).

8. End Times Stats,
   http://www.liferesearchuniversal.com/etstats1.html (accessed July 2, 2008).

9. USGS, *Historic Worldwide Earthquakes: Sorted by Magnitude, Magnitude 6.0 and Greater*,
   http://earthquake.usgs.gov/regional/world/historical_mag_big.php (accessed July 2, 2008).

10. Scott Ashley, *Does the Bible Predict Storms Like Katrina for the End Time?*
    http://www.ucg.org/commentary/predictstorms.htm (accessed July 2, 2008).

11. ibid.

12. ibid.

13. Discovery News, *Natural Disasters Four Times More Common*,
    http://dsc.discovery.com/news/2007/11/26/natural-disasters-warming.html (accessed July 2, 2008).

14. *2004 Indian Ocean earthquake*,
    http://en.wikipedia.org/wiki/2004_Indian_Ocean_earthquake (accessed July 2, 2008).

15. *2005 Atlantic hurricane season*,
    http://en.wikipedia.org/wiki/2005_Atlantic_hurricane_season (accessed July 2, 2008).

16. *Hurricane Katrina*,
    http://en.wikipedia.org/wiki/Hurricane_Katrina (accessed July 2, 2008).

17. Planet Ark, *Natural Disasters Will Increase - UN Meteorologists*,
    http://www.planetark.com/dailynewsstory.cfm/newsid/40951/story.htm (accessed July 2, 2008).

18. B. Raman, *Indonesian terror group wants to establish Islamic Caliphate in South East Asia*, October 14, 2002,
    http://www.rediff.com/news/2002/oct/14raman.htm (accessed July 2, 2008).

19. Western Resistance, Indonesia: *Did Muslims Behead Three Christian Girls?*
    http://www.westernresistance.com/blog/archives/000722.html (accessed July 2, 2008).

20. CNN.com, Transcripts, *Interview With Joel Osteen*, Aired June 20, 2005,
    http://transcripts.cnn.com/TRANSCRIPTS/0506/20/lkl.01.html (accessed July 2, 2008).

21. U.S. Department of Defense, *Sustaining Flight Through Knowledge* (Remarks of Paul G. Kaminski),
    http://www.defenselink.mil/speeches/speech.aspx?speechid=963 (accessed July 2, 2008).

Chapter Nine: Decoding the End-Times Beast

1. Main Events in the History of Jerusalem,
   http://www.centuryone.com/hstjrslm.html (accessed July 2, 2008).

2. ibid.

3. Broad Wall, *Hezekiah prepares for the Assyrian assault*,

http://www.biblewalks.com/Sites/BroadWall.html (accessed July 2, 2008).

4. Michael Fortner, *The Scarlet Beast* (Lawton, OK: White Stone press, 2006). p. 6
5. ibid. p. 5
6. ibid. p. 6
7. ibid. p. 12
8. ibid.
9. ibid. p. 13
10. ibid. p. 15
11. ibid. p. 6
12. ibid. p. 16
13. ibid.

Chapter Ten: The Awakening of the Beast

1. Daniel Pipes, *Turkey, Still a Western Ally?* Jerusalem Post, http://www.meforum.org/article/pipes/5180 (accessed July 2, 2008).
2. *Turkey-United States relations*, http://en.wikipedia.org/wiki/Turkey-United_States_relations (accessed July 2, 2008).
3. George S. Hishmeh, *Turkey's ripple effect*, GulfNews.com, September 5, 2007, http://archive.gulfnews.com/articles/07/09/06/10151632.html (accessed July 2, 2008).
4. Zehra Ayman and Ellen Knickmeyer, *Ban on Head Scarves Voted Out in Turkey*, Washington Post Foreign Service, February 10, 2008, http://www.washingtonpost.com/wp-dyn/content/article/2008/02/09/AR20 08020900832.html (accessed July 2, 2008).
5. ibid.
6. George S. Hishmeh, *Turkey's ripple effect*, GulfNews.com, September 5, 2007, http://archive.gulfnews.com/articles/07/09/06/10151632.html (accessed July 2, 2008).
7. ibid.
8. ibid.
9. Soner Cagaptay, *Turkish Secularism is Withering*, Newsweek International, September 3, 2007, http://www.washingtoninstitute.org/templateC06.php?CID=1081 (accessed July 5, 2008).
10. Yigal Schleifer, *Looking to Mideast, not West, Turkey plays role of mediator*, JTA, November 12, 2007, http://www.jta.org/cgi-bin/iowa/news/article/20071113turkeyisrael.html (accessed July 2, 2008).
11. ibid.
12. Peter Hirschberg, *Israel and Syria Flirt with Détente*, Antiwar.com,

http://www.antiwar.com/orig/hirschberg.php?articleid=12646 (accessed July 2, 2008).

13. Aaron Klein, *Israel won't press Syria to cut Iran, terrorist ties*, WorldNetDaily, May 28, 2007, http://www.wnd.com/index.php?pageId=64899 (accessed July 2, 2008).

14. Peter Hirschberg, *Israel and Syria Flirt with Détente*, Anti war.com, http://www.antiwar.com/orig/hirschberg.php?articleid=12646 (accessed July 2, 2008).

Chapter Eleven: Testing the Theory

1. Muhammed and the Treaty of Hudaybiyya, http://www.answeringislam.info/Muhammad/hudaybiyya.html (accessed July 2, 2008).

Chapter Twelve: Unmasking the Mahdi

1. Walid, *Islam and the Final Beast*, http://www.answering-islam.org/Walid/gog.htm (accessed July 2, 2008).

2. Gary Stearman, *Israel, Iran, the Bomb And the Spring Equinox – Nuclear Weapons: Primed, Aimed and Ready!* Prophecy in the News, http://www.prophecyinthenews.com/articledetail.asp?Article_ID=194 (accessed July 2, 2008).

3. Mufti A.H. Elias and Mohammad Ali ibn Zubair Ali, *Imam Mahdi (Descendent of Prophet Muhammad PBUH)*, http://www.islam.tc/prophecies/imam.html (accessed July 2, 2008).

4. Black Banners Will Establish Power for Mahdi [a.s], http://alkhilafah.net/victoriousarmy.html (accessed July 2, 2008).

5. Joel Richardson, *Antichrist: Islam's Awaited Messiah* (Enumclaw, WA: Pleasant Word, 2006). p. 64

6. Identification of the Prophesied Imam Mahdi, *Tirmidhi Sahih, Vol. 9, P. 74; Abu Dawud, Sahih, Vol. 5, P. 207*; http://www.irshad.org/islam/prophecy/mahdi.htm (accessed July 2, 2008).

7. WorldNetDaily, *Iran Leader's Messianic End-times Mission*, January 6, 2006, http://www.worldnetdaily.com/news/article.asp?ARTICLE_ID=48225 (accessed July 2, 2008).

Chapter Thirteen: The Mark of the Beast

1. Walid Shoebat, *Why I Left Jihad* (Top executive Media, 2005). p.321
2. ibid. p. 321
3. ibid. p. 320
4. ibid.

5. ibid. p. 321
6. ibid. p. 320
7. ibid.
8. ibid. p. 322

Chapter Fourteen: The Islamic Revival: What in the World is Happening?

1. Samuel P. Huntington, *The Age of Muslim Wars*,
   http://www.hvk.org/articles/1003/48.html (accessed July 3, 2008).
2. James Phillips, *Iraq Is a Strategic Battleground in the War Against Terrorism*, The heritage Foundation,
   http://www.heritage.org/Research/Iraq/wm1210.cfm (accessed July 4, 2008).
3. Patrick Jackson, *Who are Iraq's Mehdi Army?* BBC News, May 30, 2007,
   http://news.bbc.co.uk/2/hi/middle_east/3604393.stm (accessed July 3, 2008).
4. ibid.
5. ibid.
6. Timothy Furnish, *Will Iraq Stoke Flames of Islamic Messianism?* Pajamas Media, April 7, 2008,
   http://pajamasmedia.com/blog/will-iraq-stoke-flames-of-islamic- (accessed July 3, 2008).
7. Muslim Population Statistics,
   http://muslim-canada.org/muslimstats.html (accessed July 3, 2008).
8. Chad Groening, *Current birth rates could produce Muslim domination*, Free republic, February 2, 2007,
   http://www.freerepublic.com/focus/f-news/1780026/posts (accessed July 3, 2008).
9. Muslim Population Statistics,
   http://muslim-canada.org/muslimstats.html (accessed July 3, 2008).
10. Omer Taspinar, *Europe's Muslim Street*, Brookings,
    http://www.brookings.edu/opinions/2003/03middleeast_taspinar.aspx (accessed July 3, 2008).
11. ibid.
12. ibid.
13. ibid.
14. ibid.
15. ibid.
16. *2005 civil unrest in France*,
    http://en.wikipedia.org/wiki/2005_civil_unrest_in_France (accessed July 3, 2008).
17. Elaine Sciolino, *Paris suburb riots called 'a lot worse' than in 2005*, Herald Tribune, November 27, 2007,
    http://www.iht.com/articles/2007/11/27/europe/riots.php (accessed July 3, 2008).
18. Omer Taspinar, Europe's Muslim Street, The Muslim News,

November 3, 2003,
http://www.muslimnews.co.uk/news/news.php?article=4432 (accessed July 3, 2008).

19. Tony Blankley, *Will We Win the Clash of Civilizations?* The Huffington Post, September 16, 2005,
http://www.huffingtonpost.com/tony-blankley/will-we-win-the-clash-of-_b_7487.html (accessed July 3, 2008).

20. Memri, *Special Dispatch: Quotes from Saudi Cleric Nasser bin Suleiman Al-'Omar*,
http://memri.org/bin/articles.cgi?Page=archives&Area=sd&ID=SP115406 (accessed July 3, 2008).

21. History of the Middle East, *Under European Domination*,
http://en.wikipedia.org/wiki/History_of_the_Middle_East (accessed July 3, 2008).

22. Hugh Fitzgerald, *Understanding The Resurgence Of Islam*, New English Review,
http://www.newenglishreview.org/custpage.cfm/frm/8724/sec_id/8724 (accessed July 3, 2008).

23. ibid.

24. ibid.

25. ibid.

26. ibid.

27. Susan Katz Keating, *The Wahhabi Fifth Column*, FrontPageMagazine.com, December 30, 2002,
http://www.frontpagemag.com/Articles/Read.aspx?GUID=ABD54405-1F55-405D-8F0B-754FAC23C5CD (accessed July 3, 2008).

28. ibid.

29. ibid.

30. ibid.

31. ibid.

32. ibid.

33. Paul Landau, *Hamas and Islamic Millenarianism: What the West Doesn't Recognize*, World Politics Review, January 8, 2008,
http://www.worldpoliticsreview.com/Article.aspx?id=1481 (accessed July 3, 2008).

34. ibid.

35. ibid.

36. ibid.

Chapter Fifteen: The Reach of the Beast: How Will America be Affected?

1. It's all about Iraq, isn't it?
http://thereligionofpeace.com/ (accessed July 3, 2008).

2. James S. Robbins, *The Voice of Osama*, National Review Online, October 7, 2002,

http://www.nationalreview.com/robbins/robbins100702.asp (accessed July 3, 2008).

3. Bay Fang, *U.S. torn in clash between Turkey and Iraq*, Chicago Tribune.com, October 17, 2007, http://www.swamppolitics.com/news/politics/blog/2007/10/us_to rn_in_clash_between_turke.html (accessed July 3, 2008).

The Islamic Ottoman Empire, Circa 1680